kierkegaard
A FICTION

SYRACUSE UNIVERSITY PRESS   1974

kierkeGaard
A FICTION

BARBARA ANDERSON

Library of Congress Cataloging in Publication Data

Anderson, Barbara Carol, 1943-
    Kierkegaard.

Includes bibliographical references.
1. Kierkegaard, Søren Aabye, 1813-1855 — Fiction.
PZ4.A5447Ki [PS3551.N357] 813'.5'4 74-7861
ISBN O-8156-0100-X

Manufactured in the United States of America

To John: Who alone is better than possibility

Barbara Anderson received the B.A. degree from Hunter College in 1963 and the M.A. and Ph.D. in Philosophy from The Pennsylvania State University in 1966 and 1967. She has taught philosophy at Skidmore College and The Pennsylvania State University and now devotes her time to teaching English and writing. Her articles on Kierkegaard and art have appeared in literary and philosophical journals.

CONTENTS

Foreword   ix

Sigh of Fire   1

Letter to R   3

Editor's Note to His Mother's Diary   11

Editor's Note to a Prostitute's Will   45

Editor's Note to Regine's Tale   77

Editor's Note to the Letters of "That Single Individual"   121

Editor's Final Note   145

Notes   151

This book is wholly fiction.

The Publisher

FOREWORD

If my memory of the past seven years is correct, I have taught only one course devoted exclusively to Soren Kierkegaard, and that one not by my own choice but because it was my turn to teach in the "Great Philosophers" series and Kierkegaard's turn to be taught. Were it necessary for me to identify myself with one or another philosopher or philosophical movement, it would be a long while before I should even consider Kierkegaard or existentialism. Thus, it is most strange that I find myself involved with the publication of this particular manuscript. For this work, which I have spent many months pondering and over two years trying to publish, is about Kierkegaard. Moreover, the events leading to my involvement with it — to the exclusion of my other professional obligations — are equally strange.

To make certain that I do not distort the story, I have consulted the daily journal which it has been my habit to keep for the past ten years. On Friday, the sixth of July, 1970, I recorded the following:

9:30 P.M. I am seated at my work table in a cottage on the outskirts of Copenhagen — at the edge of a forest. I am here to make a holiday of the last two months of my sabbatical leave, too much of which has been spent in Berlin! Sigrid Lund arranged the rental. She says it has a tradition of being occupied by writers and artists. I can see why. The countryside is quite picturesque: a rolling meadow scalloped with beeches and evergreens. The interior of the cottage is startlingly simple. The walls are in part of rough wood, in part of rough-hewn logs; and the floors are planks of oak, I think. A long, narrow rug of a flat weave, in broad stripes of faded blues, trails down the center of the main room. An oil lamp with a flat hood hangs above me; and five feet away, a candle dish with a delicate stencil of berries sits on a low, square table. Three tall, narrow windows, unbleached curtains hanging straight down. Beside one window, a small, square mirror; and save for three bookshelves, nothing else hangs on the walls. Two tables, three straight-back wood chairs, a small, polished chest with three drawers, and a fireplace with a cooking surface and faucet. These are the downstairs furnishings. Upstairs, in the half-story bedroom, a wooden bed with a rose-colored coverlet fits in a low-ceilinged alcove. Under the narrow window is a bedside table with a candle stick and candle; a cupboard hangs from a slanted roof wall; the mirror on it shows a distorted image of the room. At the foot of the bed there are four narrow steps which lead to a crawl space. I would hardly have climbed them were I not scrupulously thorough in cleaning places I intend to inhabit for any length of time. Besides, I am something of a prowler when alone in a new location. The crawl space, unlike the rooms below, was dusty and smelled of mulch. I pushed some of the dust into one corner with my brush, and wiped the floor with my cloth. I found a bundle of candle ends of various lengths tied together with string; a pile of small twigs, apparently kindling; and another small bunch of dried grass and seed pods. Behind these, bound with some sort of ribbon, I noticed a stack of old papers. I crawled in and retrieved them, my curiosity and interest in detail getting the best of me. They are here upon this table. I have not yet untied the ribbon, but I can read the first page which says "SIGH OF FIRE." This is Kierkegaard's phrase as I recall. Below this page, is a letter to "R" who is apparently an editor. My guess is that I have found a manuscript which has something to do with Kierkegaard. However, I am too tired from the day's travel, unpacking, and cleaning to examine it now with the necessary care. It is 10:00 — too late for reading even under ordinary circumstances!

My journal can be relied upon as an impeccable source of detail. I note, however, that with respect to this particular event, it fails to reflect anything of the unusual sense of excitement I felt, even in its tone! But from the detail, at this moment, I immediately recapture the thrill of my discovery, my hope that I had inadvertently come upon an unknown manuscript by Kierkegaard. Despite my curiosity and excitement, the small, hard bed lured me into a sleep uneasy with anticipation. As I sat drinking my first cup of coffee the following morning, I imagined myself translating the work into English and writing a final, decisive commentary.

To ensure accuracy in my report of what followed, I again quote my journal:

9:30 P.M. Saturday, July 7, 1970

It was a chilly, damp morning. Perhaps I am unused to waking in real silence. Though I did wish for something different from a city hotel, I did not anticipate so primitive a setting as this. Well, I may come to like this cottage after a bit; if nothing else, the manuscript I found here last evening is redeeming. Soon after drinking coffee and smoking the first one in a new box of Tia Havanas, I read it through, anxious to know what I had found. Almost at once, I realized that the piece was not written by Kierkegaard at all. I was disappointed. Then, angry. I felt tricked. Nonetheless, there was something compelling about the work; reading it made me feel somewhat less alone; and it was interesting, because about Kierkegaard. It is an odd work all the same, and I am not at all sure that I understand its theme, since this seems to be formulated imaginatively. I believe I shall smoke one more cigarillo and retire for the evening.

My journal shows that I did not succeed in retiring that night, but rose again, and then again.

11:16 P.M. Saturday, July 7, 1970

SIGH OF FIRE was obviously written in a kind of intoxication. The author, a woman named "Carla," is too imaginative to be a scholar or professional philosopher; yet she knows too much to be merely a writer. This is a presumptuous account by any standards! The more I think about it, the more offended I become by this "editor" who calls herself a "lover" of Kierkegaard! In a letter to someone called "R," she claims to be led almost magically to a place where some manuscripts lie buried! She finds them in various stages of decay — a deathbed diary kept by Kierkegaard's mother, the last will and testament of a prostitute whom Kierkegaard may or may not have visited, a re-telling of the story of Alaeddin's Wonderful Lamp by Regine (Kierkegaard's true love), and some letters from a "reader" of Kierkegaard's works! Guided, she says, by love for Kierkegaard, Carla edits these documents, admitting in each case to destroying the personalities of the original writers! No editor should change historical documents so that her personality replaces that of the writer. This is to treat history as romance!

1:21 A.M. Sunday, July 8, 1970

Still, the "editor" knows a good deal about Kierkegaard. Why won't she stick to the facts of his life? Or if a biography is not the point, why won't she present a clear philosophical or theological argument? There is some point to this work. WHAT is it!? Tomorrow (rather, later on this day) I shall go to the Royal Library and see if I can identify Carla, the "author-editor."

Late in the afternoon of July 8, 1970, I went to the Royal Library. In fact, I spent my entire two-month "vacation" commuting to Copenhagen, consulting the archives of Kierkegaard's works, as well as the literature about him, in a frenetic effort to find a key to the theme of the manuscript and to the identity of Carla. Though I was unable to find a single reference to a Carla in Kierkegaard's own writings, those of his biographers, his disciples, critics, or those even indirectly concerned with him, I did learn something about Kierkegaard's life and writing and *its* relation to Carla's work. Gradually, I came to the conclusion that SIGH OF FIRE was romantic fiction — a freely composed biography of Kierkegaard based upon a thorough familiarity with his works, focused by a camera obscura into four episodes in his life — episodes, I might add, which are by no means established, and in three cases are usually offered as little more than guesses by his biographers.

It is a scholarly consensus that Kierkegaard never mentions his mother in his works. Thus, the "self-portrait" of his mother which Carla presents must have been based upon the considerable amount known about Kierkegaard's relation with his father. From this information, Carla spins out many pages detailing a less-than-satisfactory relationship to his mother. So far as I can find out, nothing is really known about an episode with a prostitute, a Fall in Kierkegaard's youth, which Carla develops extravagantly into a hypnotic little piece of melodrama. Not one writer about Kierkegaard is willing to say for certain that such a Fall took place! Furthermore, Regine, whose actual history is reasonably well known, was obviously a naive, rather domestic young girl; and despite Kierkegaard's efforts to educate her, she hardly possessed the intellectual cleverness and sensitivity needed to write the symbolic allegory which Carla attributes to her.

Of course, Kierkegaard found it necessary to use pseudonyms; by endowing each of his alter-egos with its own stylistic persona, Kierkegaard himself could be removed from his own work. Carla seems to have tried to use Kierkegaard's device; but if this was her intention, I believe she was not successful. *Her* persona dominates each of the four characters. She has a poetically self-conscious voice which is far too clever and rich to represent the dying words of Kierkegaard's mother — a simple kitchen maid — or the level of culture of Regine, or the vindictive suicide letter of a prostitute. These and other scholarly inconsistencies were, and still are, exasperating! On four occasions I concluded that Carla's work was just another one of innumerable amateurish pieces on Kierkegaard which, at best, might be useful to introduce students in a gymnasium to such ideas as "anxiety," "dread," "existence." Once, I even re-wrapped it and almost mailed it to the Kierkegaard Institute. Yet, however many times I put the manuscript aside, I could not dismiss it. I was continually haunted by Carla's obvious intimacy with Kierkegaard's life and thought and the intoxication so evident in her work. I could not help but feel that my scholarly observations were irrelevant to the real insight of SIGH OF FIRE.

Perhaps it was the evident impact of Kierkegaard on Carla that committed me to try to arrange for the publication of her work. She does not reflect Kierkegaard's work or life so much as Kierkegaard the man! In her writing, I did not recognize the Kierkegaard of scholars and theologians. The Kierkegaard reflected through the four characters was an unattractive even hateful man — but a real one! Though it is difficult for me to maintain this subjective frame and meet Kierkegaard the man within, it is the only frame which makes the manuscript meaningful. Read as Carla's response to Kierkegaard himself, her manuscript no longer makes a claim to represent his life or works, but becomes an impassioned argument with him through the voices of four characters.

If the book is to be judged as romantic fiction, I can only observe that from a literary standpoint, the manuscript is very uneven. There are passages that are quite brilliantly written, some that are nicely written and many that are overwritten, flat and strained. Yet if Carla is responding to Kierkegaard directly, and on the basis of her radical subjectivity, her work is not romantic fiction. Some other standards of interpretation and judgment are needed.

What standards? So far as I can judge, this is neither a work of art nor a convincing philosophical revelation nor a thorough and penetrating biography of Kierkegaard. Measured thus, it is, I think, a pretentious failure. I do not feel comfortable with the methods of the author or with the Kierkegaard who emerges through their use. Were I to write a book on this philosopher, I could not pursue so unscholarly a path, nor could I develop such an unattractive image of him — of any philosopher! As my involvement with this work deepened, I tried making revisions: modifying the style to eliminate extravagance and unnecessary floridity, experimenting with returning to the four characters their *propria personae* in accordance with what is historically known of them. I even tried eliminating the deliberate enigmas, symbolic contrivances, and the persistent intrusion of the "author-editor" throughout. For some time, I have had on my desk two versions of the manuscript: Carla's and the one resulting from my revisions. Each time I read my version, I prefer Carla's for its originality, ambitiousness, and boldness, even though these are precisely the virtues which had kept me from committing myself publicly to it.

Though this is not a book I would write, it is a book which I have come to accept as significant in its own terms — one which thus ought to be published largely in its original form. I have even decided to include the curious letter to "R" which accompanied the manuscript. Besides this brief Foreword, I have supplied quotations at the beginning of each set of papers and a number of notes at the end which I believe will help the reader recognize the intricate relationship between this work and Kierkegaard's life and works. But my support of Carla's work is compelled less by its scholarly competence than by a deep obligation I feel to Carla, who was, as an individual, able to find Kierkegaard the man, and to respond to him.

B. C. Anderson

State College, Pennsylvania
Spring 1974

sigh of fire

So it was with the Titans, didn't they, too, succumb to the masses? And yet — and this is the only comfort remaining! — didn't they now and then frighten the hottentots who trot over them by drawing in a deep breath and expelling a glowing sigh of fire, not in order to complain, no, all condolence refused — but in order to terrify.

CONCEPT OF IRONY, *p. 24.*

Dear R:

I cannot come up with an acceptable explanation for being so dilatory about renewing our correspondence. I regret to say that since we last spoke, nothing of consequence has come of my work at the Library, which has largely been an uneventful tidying up of the Kierkegaard collection. And my personal life, work? Well, in anticipation of a long period of being for once on my own payroll, I postponed doing any of the things there was only me to do — to want to do. But now I have reason to write. I have a manuscript for you! And if there should be any of your old, wholly unjustified generosity toward me left after these few years, I wish above all to have your influence in getting my manuscript published by your Press.

We must meet again soon to talk about it — perhaps next time I am in Berlin we can dine? — then I shall give you all the answers to the riddles in the work. But for now, I shall tell you something of its extraordinary history!

Last year, as you may have guessed, I retired with the firm and final decision to begin a different sort of life. I must confess that it quite unsettled me to leave the secure world of letters where I surely had a good, solid reputation and could have thrived for many more years. Unsettling to say the least! Retirement meant becoming rather like a mermaid, a tail replacing my legs; and me, flopping around, muscles learning to supply the place of the missing limbs. Can you imagine me — in such a transition! I had to do something drastic. All I could think to do was to leave the city at once to try growing my country legs at the summer cottage I loved so well — you know, the one you visited just on the outskirts of Gribs Forest?[1] My habit was, of course, to take two or three volumes of Kierkegaard with me wherever I went! But I determined to leave all that behind. As added insurance, I took no books at all — just a drawing tablet, some pastels, and a camera, thinking to make a summer of sketching and photography. How feeble it all looks now!

Here I am, in the same cottage, now winter, still at work on Kierkegaard! My tablet bears no glimpses of this now dark, slow land, but rather words about one of its sons. And my camera — it is still unloaded, a rosewood box having taken its place. This remarkable box! It is filled with papers about Kierkegaard; not written, but collected by him, I am sure. This is the treasure I found in the woods a year ago, maybe more. It was quite extraordinary, really it was . . . I mean the way I came upon it.

It was only the third day of the vacation with which my retirement began. A late afternoon, the first Sunday in July. I wandered out of my cottage for some air. Having no particular goal, the forest, which lay not more than 50 yards before me, looked inviting. It seemed somehow suspended in space, above the dazzling green meadow. Entranced, I moved toward it — onto a rocky footpath which led around a curve. As I made the turn, I was engulfed by sweet, heavy vapors and masses of tall, grey-white beeches. Intoxicating! My knees buckled under the glare and I seemed on the verge of losing myself. Then, suddenly, I stumbled and fell.

My legs — still hardly country legs! — struck a cold,

rough stone, a monument half-embedded in the earth. Did
we venture into this wood when you were here? You, of
all, would not have forgotten such a place had you seen it.
The vapors steamed off like blown fog to reveal the monument (which might have been a meteor from the heavens)
and six paths beside my own! Seven paths into a circle —
paths like the irregular cracks from a celestial crash,
climbed from deep below the nook, and fell back from it
into seven endless ravines. I turned to look back, only to
see the depth of my own path. You know my timidity in
the woods — how even the crack of a twig turns me cold.
Yet, remarkably, I felt neither lost nor afraid. The nook
held me. It seemed the protective grove of some spiritual
force, enclosing me, focusing my awareness upon the central stone, warming, and welcoming me as hitherto only
you, and a very few kindred spirits like yourself, have.

I bent over the rock which was the focus of this
warmth; but it offered no sign, only the uneven, opaque
surface. I reached out and touched it — rough and cold —
and it moved slightly. I pushed at the point where the
earth met the base of the stone, and it rolled free! There,
in a shallow hole — a warped rosewood box wrapped in an
oiled scarf of red silk.[2] "A treasure!" I exclaimed. And it
was, believe me! I grant you it all sounds improbable, yet
you must believe!

Exhumed, the old box looked quite like those which
hold duelling pistols. I picked it up and held it to my chest
as if it were some lost and frightened child; then shaking
with excitement, I sped back to the cottage. The darkness
of that late afternoon was so intense that I must have used
powers reserved to the blind for the journey. But no extraordinary powers were needed to open the lid. I had only

to press the tiny brass button and lift it! Can you picture me, sitting at the edge of a chair, the box open in my lap, incapable, somehow, of examining the contents! Perhaps, I thought, I stumbled into a nook which had been the scene of a duel. The antagonists having killed each other... but I was evading with romance! There was the box. Open! I unfolded a second oiled silk cloth. No pistols. Papers![3] On the top, a gilt-edged sheet of parchment[4] with a seal impress upon its upper edge; and in the middle of the page,

From One Who Was Left In A Sigh Of Fire
Upon Hearing His Lovers Vanish . . .

My response to those words was immediate. Through them (though it sounds as preposterous as anything in my tale) I heard the voice of my lover! They were Kierke-gaard's words, of course! How could I possibly be mis-taken? Mistaken about some of the most memorable? I could recognize him in a chance phrase — he whose works I have translated, he whom I have curated, interpreted, prefaced, and epilogued. It was SK. Yet there was a quality to the words on that parchment which I had never sensed before . . . a heightened intimacy. Suddenly, a new light was cast upon my professional life, my involvement with him, my obsessive concern. It had not been merely pro-fessional at all! My life's work had been merely a preface to this moment of discovery, to hearing SK's explicit call, and to answering him.

Such were the first words on the first page in my treas-ure box; such, the moment of revelation. There were more, many more words; words to occupy months; words buried beneath those first words. All of the papers stacked beneath that first gilt-edged page did not contain Kierkegaard's words. I am quite certain of that. I think now that the rest of the papers were written, variously, by Kierkegaard's mother, by a rejected prostitute, by his Regine, by a reader very much like you or me. As I read the words of these persons who had actually known Kierkegaard, my exuberance faded into puzzlement. The papers were damp and crumbled, naturally; but they were written on scraps, envelopes, and sheets of all sorts. They were disorganized; their content and style shifted, and though at first I thought I detected patterns and designs, the more I studied them, collated, and rearranged them, the more ambiguous they became. Finally, I concluded that Kierkegaard had collected the papers and left them for me to discover their significance. An uncomfortable certainty! Like so many others, I tried to finish my work with him and retire. This he could never permit! So fitting that he should leave me this box, never to be done with him!

Well, what was I to do? He had trapped me with a treasure any scholar would have stolen to possess, trapped me, too, in the effort of trying to determine the precise nature and extent of its value! No, he was not about to make it easy for me to be done. I was set the new task of learning who the authors were, what significance they had for Kierkegaard, and he for them. I had only decaying, moist corpses thrown together in a box to work with! After I had answers to those questions, I had still to learn what fate Kierkegaard intended for me. What sort of trap would his treasure become, now that I had possession of it?

For many months I tried to decide what to do with these papers, focused always on the problem which Kierkegaard was (and intended to be!) for every single person who came to be intimately aware of him. Here in this packet, you will find the result of my labors. You are the first and only person to see it; for I do regard you with special fondness. You know something of Kierkegaard, something of me, and something of my odd involvement with him. I now recall those searching questions of yours. Did you guess that I was long ago in love? Save that for another time and letter, perhaps!

For now, I know that you will take me seriously, that I can dare to say to you that I have completed the speech Kierkegaard left incomplete, the speech he began in the act of collecting the papers — not really papers, but stutterings and harmonics. I have worked in this one room, worked sometimes in a frenzy, to make these fragments a song. Can I presume to say that to you? It scares me a bit to say that this is *my* song. Most assuredly it is not the truest and best of which I am capable; this is my first try at such a thing! Even my best should probably not be sufficient. But for me it is too late for delay. Too late already? Well, it is yours to have the first say. Will you dare to read it? Then will you dare to tell me that there is someone besides myself who believes that I have finished my work with Kierkegaard by having loved him.

As ever yours,
Carla

1797 — 1835

But Sarah had no blame attaching to her, she is cast forth as a prey to every suffering, and in addition to this has to endure the torture of pity — for even I who admire her more than Tobias loved her, even I cannot mention her name without saying, 'Poor girl.'

FEAR AND TREMBLING, *p. 114.*

Editor's Note to His Mother's Diary

The following papers, which appear in diary form, were, of all the manuscripts I found, in the most fragmented and incomplete form. In fact, most of what appears here is the result of my own reconstructive efforts. Restoring this set of papers has taken more time and involved more emotional strain than any of the others; indeed I cannot, at the present moment, think of any other task I have ever performed which has been so deeply painful.

The author of this fractured diary wrote with one exception upon scraps of paper torn from every available place but from a writing tablet. Some of the scraps were scarred here and there with burns; some were practically worn through with crumpling; some bore stains recognizable as blood; some were studded with clear incrustations of tears; and others bore the impress of wholly unrecognizable markings. Paradoxically, the very inconsistency of the papers, of the handwriting, the mood of the writer, the purpose of the enterprise, constituted the very consistency I needed to begin to put them together. Unlike the restorer who begins his task by selecting from the ruins those fragments which are preserved most intact, those which are most suggestive of the whole, I had to make my way through the ruins picking out the least recognizable pieces, the tiniest, most obscure scraps. One of these fragments, the only piece of writing paper I found, bore some words which I took to express the intent of the writer; and I have used these words as a guide for my reconstruction. On a torn sheet of linen, yet in a clear and steady hand, appeared this:

> But I am what I am in spite of — or is it because of — all that I have given away, all that I have lost, all, perhaps that I have sacrificed. If ever, for the purposes of naming my disease, the coroner should perform an autopsy, I wish only that he may find the broken heart of a mother.

These are rather unlikely words for a simple kitchen maid to have written; nonetheless, I have assumed that only Kierkegaard's mother could have written them. I have tried to reconstitute her diary in the spirit of these words, guided by the conviction that disease and imminent death have strange, unpredictable effects — even upon apparently simple souls. In her diary, kept during her long, fitful illness, Kierkegaard's mother recorded the events and qualities of her last months of life, as well as her recollections of the past. Through this indirect means, I believe that she attempted to alter the relationship between herself and her son.

Considering its themes and intentions, I have referred her writing to the years 1797 and 1835. It was during this period of thirty-eight years that Michael Pederson Kierkegaard, his first wife having died childless after two years of marriage, married Ane Sorensdatter Lund, previously a maid in the house, before the period of mourning was over. In 1813, Soren Aabye Kierkegaard was born, seventh and last child. In 1819, Soren Michael Kierkegaard died of "nerve disease" at twelve years of age; in 1822, Maren Kristine died of "convulsions" at twenty-five years of age. Of the year 1823, SK wrote, "But to God all things are possible. From now on, humanly speaking, I must not only be said to be running into uncertainty, but to be going to certain destruction — and in confidence in God, that is victory. That is how I understood life when I was ten years old, hence the terrible polemic that filled my soul." In 1832, Maren Kristine Kierkegaard died in childbirth at thirty-three years; in 1833, Niels Andreas died at twenty-four years of age; in 1834 Petrea Kierkegaard died in childbirth at thirty-three years of age, and Kierkegaard's mother finally died after a long illness. And in 1835 SK wrote, "Then it was that the great earthquake occurred, the terrible revolution which suddenly forced upon me a new and infallible interpretation of all the facts. Then I suspected that my father's great age was not a divine blessing, but a curse."

These events of significance, having their own peculiar bearing (or lack of it) upon his mother's writing, I include for your information — to make of them, in interpreting the relationship between her and SK what you will.

The first day, 1834

So. Here I lie with a pen in my hand. Strange, indeed. Yet there is nothing left to do but this. To write.

What it is that plagues my body and drives me continually back to my doom — this bed of death — I think I know. The doctor, as usual, speaks only in the vaguest of terms. What does he know of my singularly human disease? He is in the wrong branch of medicine for it. "At what place, exactly, is it you are suffering," says he. "In all places, everywhere, dear Doctor."[5] "Everywhere? But what does this mean?" He approaches his manuals on everywhere; and he points his finger slowly down the revered list: "Fever? None. Heart? Regular. Lungs? Normal. Cheeks? Full, pink. Disposition? Good. Pain? Mild, . . ." and so on, up and down, he checks and rechecks everything . . . everywhere! Charming doctor! How serious you are in your measured pacing, believing with misplaced faith that something, *something* must show up! Good doctor; this is an illness with no symptoms — no appearance. How then can there be a name for it in your manuals? "Very suspect," you say. "An illness without a name!" The patient must surely die but for the discovery of a name, perhaps even one of those very impressive Latin ones! If you could hear me doctor, I, an uneducated servant, could whisper its name to you, for I know it. If you could sit patiently by my side while I die of it, you might learn something of this exotic plague. But to do so, you must approach my cell as a priest, or something of the kind; and this is impossible.

I fear the worst. No. I welcome it. What I fear is that I shall not be capable of speech, that I shall be permanently abandoned, left with silence as a last companion. I have lived too long shut up with silence.[6] It hovers on the brink of overtaking me. The scraps of my "position" were once enough to save me. Sweeping the floor and checking the day's menu permitted speech. There was the speech of daily prayer, the speech of acceding to demands, the speech of "Good-morning-and-good-evening," and the speech of useless, rhetorical questions. All of this speaking was authorized by my "position" in the house of Michael Pederson Kierkegaard. But now I am unable to engage in the sweeping, the cooking, the religious exercises, the charade of good-morning-and-good-day. No sooner do I rise from my bed to repeat the movements than I am driven back to it by the heavy, mysterious refusals of my body. My strength fragments; and with my weary attachment to my bed, my "position" disappears. With it goes speech. Am I now to be left in my changed sheets, in sheets of breathless silence? Is this the final phase of life for me?

It shall not be so. For too many years my every movement was a response to a demand, to be best carried through in silence. To sum up — I have served! But the silent servant learns a great deal and, in virtue of this, often manages to put her master in bondage. I have no desire to do this; even so, I have not the strength. For the strength which permits the shift in role is the strength to reveal the silence by continuing to maintain it, and, in this way, to become a perpetual threat to the master. No. I have no longer the strength for silence, nor the desire for it. I must speak.

But, to whom? About what? Why? What are better answers than these — that I have failed to be what I am, so I must try to become this; that I have refused the revelation of what I already understand, and I must disclose it; that I have been unable to utter with my voice the words which my lips form, and I must speak them before it is too late for speech. And my speech must carry these awesome tasks through to someone in particular whom I want to know and whom I want to know me. Will this work? Is it believable?

In these last days, with paper and pen, can I come to know you any better than this — than to say that you came into this world an illegitimate child? Shall my scribblings leer back at me as so much mere colored pulp? But do I dare dismiss this last questionable path to you? The thief, time, has stolen the possibility of knowing you in the virginal sense due every child. So, you are totally lost to me. But even time cannot be blamed for it all, then and now. Between us stretches the infinite space of that guilty silence. And though we shall never be fully able to close the distance, I might still try to speak, and in my speech — which I must recognize can never substitute for knowing you — to repay you for the silence of not knowing you. At least, in the strands of recollection[7] I might offer you your childhood from afar, and thus come finally to be what I have yearned to be.

Dear Lord, may it be that in Your Infinite Wisdom and Grace You have strengthened my soul with the powers You have taken from my body; to give voice not to my limbs but to my lips; to focus my soul not upon the futility of the past but upon the hope of the future. Dear Lord, I am weak and need Your help. Help this voice, which has been so long stilled, to speak.

The second day, 1834

This morning I woke with a sense of exuberance. I felt quite as if I were able to resume my duties at double-tempo. I was convinced that the temporary infirmity had passed, and the strength needed to dispel it empowered me ever so much more than before. For a moment, while preparing my morning tub, I remembered yesterday's writing and went quickly to my bedside table to confirm its reality. There it was — a torn piece of brown paper with words scrawled unevenly, in rows which went every which way. I was both embarrassed and puzzled by the look of it. So I lighted a candle and studied it, asking myself if I really could have penned something as careless as this. But, were there any doubts that I had, its contents dispelled them. It was as if I were reading about a secret, deliberately concealed dimension of myself that only someone else would be willing to put into print. But I had to admit that only I could have had access to the realities to which the words referred.

I was shocked by the futility and despair in it. Me! Such a cheerful person, sounding so morbid! I must really have been in a fit of melancholy! So I resolved, somewhat flippantly, to give some further thought to the peculiar document — perhaps, even at some later date, to retrieve it from my bedside drawer and make some further effort at writing. So went my evaluation of the day past.

But this was a new day; and I was feeling quite energetic. My tub ready, I bent my head over toward the wash basin, and began routinely to splash my face. But so soon as the water made contact with my skin, all of the blood in my head and all of the warm life I took so much for granted washed away. I collapsed upon the floor. Michael Pederson tells me that I gave the children quite a start, and you in particular, as you were just departing for the university. I have been conscious now for a few hours, and feel as if I have been submerged in deep waters too long. Despite my protestations, the doctor has been summoned once more, and I am once again thrown back upon myself and upon the document I too prematurely replaced in my bedside drawer. I am not to be so easily released from this writing . . . this, perhaps my final speech . . . my final battle with silence?

I am no authority on the subject. And even with my nominal role, my physical connections, I must still speak without authority;[8] otherwise, I would not need to speak at all. So I write without authority when I say that you were born the youngest and also the oldest child. You were born the last child who was granted the clear heritage of childhood, but also the first child who ever lived. You were a child who had ample resources for imitating childhood; and yet you were a child who had to create your childhood from the future. You were really not a child at all. To this I can attest.

I can recall your silence as a baby, and your glance which was frightfully calm. It was unnecessary for you to gain attention through shouts and demands made more urgently than the rest. The sharpness of your presence was keenly expressed in your silence. There in a cradle, or cradled in my arms, you were the apparently calm eye of the hurricane — seeming to be nothing at all in yourself but the balance of all the chaotic forces of our household. But the virgin hurricane moving onto land from its life at sea loses its precision and melts into rainshowers and winds. As you grew from infancy, you had to learn what no legitimate child needs to learn. You had to learn the immediacy of love with nothing but abstract reflection.[9] Your childhood was not to be a straining forward out of the innocence of the senses toward more and more indirect satisfactions, but a straining backward[10] from reflection toward love simultaneously needed and received. My poor child! Even hurricanes can rarely return to the sea but instead are shipwrecked on those inevitable shores which surround them. I do not think that whatever fragments of love were yours as a child were corrupted fully into wind and rain in the years spent in the house of your father. But surely these were the years of passage from sea to shore.

The very thought of these years lies heavy on my mind, which is itself still liquid like the sea. Those years float upon it like a mass of tiny puzzle pieces, none of which is distinctive enough to hold any clue about the whole, no two of which seem to fit together. Again, my strength seems to be fragmenting. Today I have not the patience needed to start sorting the pieces.

The seventh day, 1834

It is four o'clock A.M. and this is the sixth maybe the
seventh time I have been awakened by the pulsing of my
own heart, the explosions in my lungs. I am terrified! They
have isolated me in the upstairs quarters . . . the place
where the servants live . . . what irony! There is a nurse in
the room adjoining mine who is to stand guard over me;
but she is evidently sound asleep. I could call out to her,
but what could she do? Besides, my terror paralyses my
voice, and the sound of my heart beating and my lungs exploding deafens me . . . can she not hear them? I manage
to sleep deeply for a short while, but then I am up with a
sense of having run many miles or having dived many
fathoms. The sleep itself is wearisome to death. I try removing my bedclothes, to sit propped up, to lie with cold
linen upon my face, but to no avail. That same dry, cold
heat returns ever more intensely — enervating me and ex-
hausting me until, somehow, unconscious forces overtake
me according to their will, and I swoon back to sleep.

So now I must wait in this fever-heated bed to be again
overcome by the devil within me. Writing seems the only
activity which does not magnify my terror nor intensify
the throbbing of my body. Whether it is the precision of
it, the projected focus of it, or the content of it, I do not
know. Perhaps it is something far different. But no matter.
I find some limited comfort in holding the pen in my
hand, in focusing upon you and trying to speak to you. As
soon as I begin to write, the muscles of my body relax,
the heat becomes a climate not within but around me, the
pulsing is absorbed into the beat of transcription, word
after word picking up my pulse and fastening it upon

paper. This writing, my labor of love, now seems to be the only sure antidote to what ails me.

Two children were dead before you were born, and two died shortly afterwards. Your father, who was in anxious waiting for God's clear response to his sins, was now certain. His dread was warranted. God had freely bestowed great fortune upon the chosen shepherd-boy only to provide him with his means to suffering.[11] God's revenge had begun. To your father, you were a bitter gift from God; a son granted in old age when new signs of blessedness should have vanished with the movement to complete one's destiny. You came as a reminder of the lust — yes, lust — which God would not permit him to forget, even in his old age; a reminder that in the incarnated soul of this newborn child was reflected his own distance from salvation. You were born as another treasure to be sacrificed and as your father's last chance for salvation. You were born as the last sign of your father's damnation; and as his last hope for redemption. And so you spent the early years of your life not in the soft embrace of playful fantasy and the nearness of warm flesh, but in the all-too-chilling atmosphere of a house ruled by a man who was beginning to feel the wrath of God and who, in despair of knowing how to respond, turned to you, his youngest child. You were to provide the last occasion for demonstrating his faith. Through the son, the father was prevented by God from growing old and forgetting the sins of youth. And the father could do nothing but become older through the son who, though born the youngest, thus became the oldest.

Why were nine months in my womb enough to make you only an old man? Why were you denied the birthgown of joy? Why were you born not only out of pain but for the sake of pain? Why were your eyes not opened for satisfaction but only to behold the world of sighs and to be unable to break loose from it?[12]

Your father found comfort in your natural silence and calm. They preserved that innocence and vulnerability which would ensure the obedience and purity of acceptance which he imagined would please God. He took pains to isolate you, to foster your silent attentiveness, to shield you from such influences as would weaken your bond with him, a bond sealed by unspoken vows of mutual devotion. How jealous I was of this exclusive intimacy between father and son; I should call it incestuous were it not for your father's continual invocation of a more absolute relationship. You had replaced me in your father's life, so that I was thrice-removed from his most intense preoccupations; and he had replaced me in your life; so that I was thrice-removed from my son's most intense needs.

Now I have grown weary of this exclusion . . . so weary that I am about to accept it; indeed, I seem even to approve it by talking to myself . . . so indirectly, that I become — through the mirage of my son — my own audience! What is happening to me, Dear God!?

The fourteenth day, 1834

The doctor no longer comes. Whether by insight or ignorance, he has appropriately resigned from my case. For my family, his absence has meant that I am no longer in the ranks of the common patient. Since my behavior is quite ordinary most of the time, I am, in one sense, treated as normal; though in quite another sense, my periodic lapses into mysterious swoons and fits have placed me in somewhat the same position as the leper who, being so totally beyond even the normal ranges of disease, is not regarded as human at all. At most, my family tolerates me in slight overtones of fearful curiosity, as if they were living with some caged exotic jungle animal.

I suppose I have given them up. All but one. Today he came to visit between classes at the university. He seemed quite perturbed. He does not know how to respond to me now; this familiar woman who was so unobtrusive, passive, and wholly untroublesome but who now expresses some horrible corruption which has no name. How is one to deal with her? Even approach her? But he is too sensitive to ignore me. He seems, for the past two weeks, to have tried, to have devoted himself to his studies as a justification and diversion. And, too, I am certain that he is deeply troubled by the distrust and anger growing between him and his father. He looks like an old man himself . . . more burdened by his body than ever before. His hair is more than usually unkempt, and he takes no pains with his dress, as was his practice.

I have been back to bed for some days now, and have been quite anxious for a visit from him. But today He stayed only briefly — staring at me quizzically, taking my hand and reporting matter of factly the major events taking place at the university. Somewhere toward the middle of the report, he became fidgety and restless, so much so that he released my hand and began to pace the floor until, very abruptly, he clapped his hands together, and with his back toward me, bade a hasty farewell. I do not think that he stopped to talk to his father at all, for within a few moments, Michael Pederson entered, asking for a report on his son's condition. This very fact is even more strange to me than my illness! Michael Pederson — the father whose relation to his children was absolute; from whom nothing was or could be hidden; the father who was more pregnant with his children than I; the father whose own life was so intricately bound up with the lives of his children that he was willing to give up all else for them — this father comes to me . . . a servant in the house . . . to learn about his dearest child.

Yes. I remember how obsessed he was with his children; with you in particular, my son. When the children began to die, he gave up his business, then he surrendered the warmth of family life, then I was to be renounced — and soon, I was certain that you were to be brought to the sacrificial altar. Slowly, your father made preparations; slowly, the lamb was being readied. At the time, I was aware of being witness to a terrible event, but I could not understand or determine its nature. I knew the magnitude of the event for certain only in the extent to which I feared being alone with you. You seemed to bear in yourself the burden of your father's salvation. You appeared as the caretaker of the old man's soul . . . a tiny priest. I have always felt uneasy in the presence of such men; and to sense you, bearing in your infancy the mighty task of spiritual shepherd, was simply terrifying.

When I, along with his business and his family, suffered sacrificial death, your father ceased speaking; and so it was not surprising that of his relationship to you he said not a word. But this made me all the more acute; and I was able to determine exactly when he shifted from being watchful to being certain. This occurred on the day Maren Kristine died. You were but ten years old. When you were but a child of four, when Soren Michael's death made him watchful, your father addressed me with the words, "You would do well to weigh your continued security and high place in society against your womanish curiosity and sentimentalism; and if you do as you should, and decide in favor of your station in life, then you shall become nothing more than a cheerful domestic in this house." When he became watchful, I began my love affair with silence. But when with Maren's death, he became certain, he said nothing at all; and I, for him, finally disappeared into silence. I was a ghost who witnessed much in the hiddenness of daylight, but when it grew dark, I was often called back to being. For I had become the ghost who haunted your father's dark hours.

It is dark now in this room, a room so distant from that dark bedroom which I haunted for so many years, that it seems another planet. Today, in this room, I had not the same sort of intercourse with your father as I have had in rooms with beds. Today, in this room, I spoke of his son, and about his son, as if only I and not his father knew him; and as if only I alone could know him. How this seemed to at once humble and irritate the father! In this room, something far different is growing and developing within me than has seven times been the result of communion with Michael Pederson. And if the Lord is willing, beyond seven to eight times, to aid and empower my labor, I shall, even in my weakest moments, once more, and in the most agonizing labor of all, give birth.

I seem to be getting better and worse at the same time. I feel more alive than I have ever felt, and also closer than ever to death. Though inquiries these days are few, I can hardly make myself intelligible to those who would ask about my condition. At most, I manage to look at them straight on and smile that all is well. I can barely interpret the situation to myself, so paradoxical does it seem. I no longer attempt anything more than brief, slow excursions from my bed to the window or to the door, to try to catch the mood of the street or the house. This morning I was actually surprised to discover snow falling; so oblivious to the actual season was I that were the question to arise, the heat of the past weeks surely would have convinced me that it was late summer.

Upon seeing the snow, a sharp chill ran through my bones, seeming to crack them into splinters as it passed. I ran, shaking all over, back to bed, and spent a very long while shivering under the down quilts, waiting for the heat to return. But I have become used to these rapid shifts in climate and temperature, and I have made use of my hard training in patience to endure them. Unfortunately, I had not recovered from this shivering before Soren arrived, unexpectedly. This was his second visit, and again, it was brief.

He burst into my room with the same restless energy he displayed during his first visit — as if the energy itself were to constitute a veil behind which he might hide. However, his agitation ceased abruptly upon sight of me smothered, in what appeared to be a convulsion, beneath the sheets. Though this was just a fit of the shivers to which I had become quite accustomed, to Soren it must have been a shocking sight; for he threw himself upon me, so that his whole body covered mine in a desperate embrace. Then he began to weep; and his weeping became so intense that he, too, began to shiver. And then he called out to me in words whose meanings I could not understand, but whose tones were unmistakably desperate and imploring. The heaviness of his body upon mine and its uncontrolled movement seemed to cure me for the moment. Indeed, the heat became quickly intolerable, and I should surely have suffocated had I not been able to shift the porous quilts about till he slipped off. He lay beside me, gasping and limp, while I reassured him and calmed his unknown, wordless fears with a mother's voice. When at last he had recovered, convinced by my voice, he rose and extinguished the flame of my bedside candle (for night was falling) and proceeded silently out of the room.

It is now quite dark, and I find myself preoccupied with the strange intimacy of this afternoon, an intimacy which I find both wholly right and intelligible, and also wholly aberrant and mysterious. Only nights have held intimacy, and then with Michael Pederson. I missed the afternoons of gentle communion with my children; afternoons something like . . . though surely not exactly like . . . this one. With us, communion had only a religious significance. Religion took the place of family picnics and visits to the country. Being a mother meant preparing the children for worship; being a father meant training the children for worship and rigors of a Christian life.

In training you in Christianity, your father was preparing you all for your own fates and preparing himself for the time when he was to become certain of his own. This father who became watchful could no longer spare himself to engage his children, each one individually, in some one or another immediate personal expression. Instead, they became, each one singly, a part of his congregation, loving him in the unison of prayer and the silence of receiving God's word. This father, who could not be spared to love each child, could be delivered back to himself through a disproportionate devotion to one child. And you were the benefactor; it was your salvation which was to authorize, indeed to constitute, your father's. Hours went by before you two would emerge from the library, before you would arrive home from a carriage ride or a walk in the woods. And your exhaustion! Your father, pale with passion! You, your back hunched in the intensity of your effort. I knew that your father, with words which had no definitions, was initiating you ever more deeply into the mysteries of his awesome religion.

The other children, with whom I could feel closer and more useful, were spared these deep burdens and found their childhood together in the innocent love of Christianity. Though you usually took part in their ceremonies, you obviously took no comfort from them and would often withdraw into such deep isolation that the group would disperse leaving you alone in your seat; or would end a prayer only to hear your small voice carrying its meanings more deeply into your soul. At other times, your participation seemed but a service to the others, your way of being their brother. But you really loved only your father.

So it went for the first four years of your life (only four!), a life accepting its place in your father's preparedness. The day Kristine died, all was ready. That day, you and your father retreated into the country together, leaving the rest of us the bare comfort of our sense of providence and each other. The children hardly noticed the retreat; they had become quite accustomed to your distant presence. But I had not; I had developed a depth of concern and sensitivity equal to your father's growing sense of certainty. Far from adapting myself to your abandonment, I felt ever more keenly the rejection in it. I reacted to it more and more sharply with the only effective response left to me: thought! I am, to this day, amazed at the extent to which I have been able to penetrate these terrible complexities through thought — relying completely on my native powers and secret trips to your father's library. My inward turmoil, as well as this development of my intellectual competence, went unnoticed by the children. They grew accustomed to my merely nominal presence, and relied upon each other, prayer and Bible-reading to provide the support and nearness which I had long ceased to provide.

Of course, since my powers of interpretation developed inwardly and in silence, I was never quite certain of the extent to which I understood things. Only now, as I write it down, am I sure of the scope and depth of my awareness and my ability to articulate it. In fact, the past itself seems to suffer an essential rebirth in the flow of ink from my pen. But still I sometimes wonder — do I view a distorted landscape from my fevered brain, as your father saw the countryside only in endless imaginative walks through his library?

A day, 1834

First the seasons disappeared; now even days are irrelevant.

Many too many days have passed, I think, and I have not
permitted a single one to disappear without writing. I
know this, because my bedside drawer is filled with papers,
filled with words. They are very peculiar documents, these
papers. Most are stained with blood. And I do not doubt
that many are stained with tears. The papers themselves
vary in quality; most are not writing paper at all but scraps
from newspapers, postcards, and food wrappings. The writing is illegible and incoherent . . . like the expectorations
of a madwoman. Periodically, I realize enough distance
from them to become astonished; but quickly, they all
seem quite normal, and my wild head-shaking becomes just
an objective confusion. I do not know what to do with
these scraps of blood and tears; they have begun to spill
out of the drawer. I am afraid lest they be discovered and
interpreted as symptoms of mere insanity. I think I shall
put most of them in the rosewood pedestal which Michael
Pederson keeps in the old attic secretary,[13] . . . perhaps to
be joined later by some more considered documents.

Soren has failed to appear in this room since that trou-
bling afternoon; and I feel, somehow, that my deteriora-
tion over the intervening weeks has been a consequence of
this experience and his absence. Why does he not come?
Perhaps my mad scribblings are so many small invitations
to him, invitations never received. Do his studies dominate
him? Is he repelled by my illness? Do I frighten him? How
can I answer these questions? Good Lord, how can I ask
them? Might he not just visit me as the duty of the son, to
sit objectively by the side of his mother? However frightened, however repelled, however preoccupied Soren has
been, he has always managed to do what he conceived was
his duty! The more inwardly perturbed his soul, the more

eloquent and natural was his outward grace.

Yes, His duty . . . why, WHY only to the Father???

Late the day of Maren Kristine's death, you and your father returned from your appointed pilgrimage. In your silent, matter-of-fact presence, you bore a resolve and focus which was buried more deeply from view with each movement you made. Neither you nor your father needed the obvious comfort we all took in mutual talk and prayer. In fact, you made no effort at all to engage in our religious exercises; nor did you appear to respond to anything except the most ordinary of topics. It was as if your souls were held fast to some post beyond the frontier of all that was human; as if to attend to anything beyond the immediacy of fact would break this tie and catapult you into chaos. I marveled at the two of you and this intricate feat performed in unison. But I also marveled at the contrast in the way each, singly, accomplished this feat. Your father seemed to be able to maintain his focus only at the cost of silence and rigidity. His behavior was blunted and mechanical; and he evaded any contact with the rest of us. But you! How graceful you were! And how skillful your manner! You even risked embellishing your presence in long monologues and idle chatter. You would drift in and out of our activities with a sort of relish and gaiety which came as close as ever to convincing me that you were really a child after all. This was the first real evidence of your mastery of deception. Were it not that I had long ago devoted myself to interpreting your behavior, I certainly would have been convinced. Instead, however, I was in awe of your courage and your self-discipline.

I knew that your father could not maintain his purity and his focus for very long. In the past, he had failed to maintain a lesser tension. But I would have staked my life on you! Of course, you were well-provided for this task with a multileveled nature and a tensile soul which could become ever more indirect without limit. For you, the immediate power of sensation was no danger; it was only a possibility — not even known to you as such. But your father knew this power, knew it as only a sinner could know it. And when he surrendered, I was there. That day of Maren's death, I anticipated the tension to break in such a way as to throw him even more sharply into sin than ever before. Then, as in the past, my dread precipitated my reincarnation. As I was to discover, you also anticipated your father's fall, but not, as I, in dread. For to you, your father's corruption was only an unknown possibility.

That dreadful night! There comes a time for each child — I remember it myself — when he confronts the incommensurable, when he discovers contradictions and formulates a distinction between the truth and lies. The crumbling of his world comes with the discovery that mother and father, the incarnations of the law,[14] lead a secret, mysterious, unjustified life. This life is buried beneath bed sheets, muffled by the dense silence of night, made mute by the language of the body alone. For the child, a new kind of suffering begins — a struggle in anxiety and wonder to shift his experiences about until they hold somehow together. But what is a child to do when his experiences carry such contradictions that he cannot hold them together, when his powers are insufficient? A father is wise to present himself to his child as a man, frail as a man, having only partial success in realizing the ideal. Then, he permits his child to understand his badly hidden secrets merely as differences, even radical differences, in his behavior. But when a father would stand before his child as the incarnation of the ideal, the space in which that child lives is reduced to an inside and an outside, and those same secrets become poles separated by an impassable gulf. Poor child! For this polarization does not merely determine his father's fate; it becomes the standard for his own. And the father's risk is that he may, at any moment, suffer the fate of the fallen idol; and the child's misfortune is that he will suffer to be dragged helplessly along.

These days you seem no longer so helpless, my child, though increasingly helpless in another sense you are most certainly becoming. There is an aura of power surrounding you, a kind of tortured assertiveness in your presence. I can only speculate as to what is preoccupying you during these long weeks of absence . . . though how I wish you would sit by me and speak of it. Your absence carries an indictment; though, strangely enough, I do not feel that it is of me you are in judgment. Even from my hidden chamber I catch the tone of this house; a ruin wherein a fallen idol broods. Your father is as rare a visitor here as his son.

1834

The torments of the sickroom! The terrors of it! The vile cancers it breeds! The insidious corruptions it fosters and hatches! This is home now, this cancerous cell shut up tight by the silence of four walls which feed only off the stagnant air grown heavy with its own isolation. The walls have only a one-sided face which looks inward toward me;

and I have grown to be their lover too, their prisoner, bound hypnotically to them by chains of narcotic air.

The corruption has invaded my body, and for want of the proper medicine, I have succumbed. I am one with the fragments of motes sluggishly thumping together in pro-creative beats, and thumping together some more. Inside, all is an amorphous mass, multiplying in an uncontrolled but not a wild way, limited by the isolating walls. How long will it go on?? Is not someone at least curious about the anomalies of the sick? I have so much that I could show, could tell!! Won't someone break through to me?? I beg you, my son . . . break down the door, burn down the walls, flood the place, cleanse the earth! It must come now from the outside. For my cries are in vain. No sooner do they leave my lips than they are washed away in up-surging blood, smothered by the air, devoured by the hungry walls, pushed back down into my lungs where they become inaudible moans; moans which, like barking dogs, last through the night. The air pushes in on me, crowding my eyelids, refusing to let them close, rushing into my head through my nostrils, coursing through my ears, ringing bells, stopping breath. My arms are buried beneath mountains of air, escaping to write only when the fog lifts them up from beneath, when the corruption changes form. I fear the end of the coming of the fog, when I shall be doomed to be buried alive under mountains of imperishable air, when I shall have everything yet to say and to be, and yet nothing left to say or to be.

No doubt, my son, you will come to save me . . . even if you come from a sense of duty. For you must know the torments of sleepless nights; you must understand by now the yearnings of a sick soul. No doubt you, yourself, had difficulty sleeping that first sleepless night. For that night underscored in black the fateful mission assigned to your single soul. You had received your commission and your sealed orders; and their magnitude must have evoked in you a watchfulness and an alertness which make for fretful nights. How the mysteries of religious duty troubled your father's sleep! How so, then, did they weigh upon your tiny soul! That your father's salvation was dependent upon your own! Of yourself, you could be sure; but what of your father? Might he be subject to some unknown, unpredictable danger? Might your place in his life include guarding his soul against such dangers? These questions, and more, must have kept you awake. And added to these questions, the weight of your sealed orders, the strength of your vows to devotion, and the shepherd's natural protectiveness of his flock, drove you to want to be near your father, drove you out of your bed, through the canyons of what was to become a vision of Hell. Not quite believing that you would find anything, not quite knowing why you were wandering through the house, not quite interested in anything, but attuned to everything, you approached the place where your father slept. Were you hoping, perhaps, just to gaze upon his face, expressing in your gaze a child's reverence and a shepherd's care? Were you hoping to be assured by the peacefulness of a soul asleep, confirming that, at least for a day, the vows taken had been carried through, and that all was well? What purity of hope you possessed! Have you none left for me now, my son?

I cannot say with assurance that you were at the door that night. What clues might there be in the dark? Even the sight of a face may be a dreaming together of inhuman images. But my complete preoccupation with you, to the exclusion of any more immediate involvements, enabled me to catch more than images. I was startled many times that night by a silent, shuffling presence, by that mixture of fear and interest which is so characteristic of children. The rhythms in which I was caught were complicated by the irregular beats of a third heart and lungs. The night air itself carried the smell of an intruder.

Your father was also wakeful. He was battling with an enemy to whom he continually surrendered. And the harder he fought, the sharper was the focus of his will upon the temptation; the more seductive the temptation became; until, in a rage of will, of obliteration of consciousness, in the onrush of the dark waves of desire, he surrendered, cursing God for refusing to allow him to grow old. And I understood him without having to ask, and without receiving explanation. I understood, too, how momentous was the day by the intensity of the Fall at night. But I did not understand just exactly how you were implicated. This night would have been like any other but for the strange presence at the door and the nature of some secret relationship which this presence signified. My tiny son . . . what brought you so close that night? While most everything in my life has faded into the dullness of routine, this riddle has pursued and obsessed me and kept me alive.[15]

Now, I am just barely alive, held in this silent world for want of an exit, so long as there is ink in my pen and fog in the mountains. Will there be enough? Enough ink, enough fog to mend the loss? All of my scraps of paper, stained in the colored inks of my body, are so many puzzle pieces, so many very temporary cures. They are yours, my son, to be put together and heard as one voice. Will you let them speak? Or will they be doomed to scream the voiceless scream of death . . . will they be forever mute? Can I manage, in the still grip of death, what I could not manage in life? Will I solve this puzzle, or shall death itself be the solution?

Here. I shall gather them all together; here, in my lap. Come, We shall listen by candle light; we shall witness their speech. Come, my son; come close to me this night. Come by the warm candle flame; no need to cringe in darkness. Come out from behind the hungry door; no need to shuffle about from one foot to the next. Come, and be close; no need to do all the work alone, to command your senses at once alive and numb. No. Come, my child. Sit upon my bed; even lie down beside me, and let us meet this human misery in our gentle embrace. Let our communion be a transformation. Let our arms extend to permit new words of love to enter this room; and let us whisper them to each other. They shall waft in upon a breeze and cause the candle to flicker ever so briefly. Will you come with them? Can you hear me, my son?

The day, 1834

A day, a year, a lifetime in a few words from my son! Only my son could have heard my singular cries. Your note came today, addressed to me. I tuck it beneath my pounding heart, my heated breast, to repose there until you take its place. You are coming! And I respond in my best words. You are coming! Tomorrow, just before dusk. I am a new woman, a bride in white. It is spring in Copenhagen; or so it shall be. I ask that the room be decked in flowers, that the shutters be thrown open, that apples be set out in bowls to reflect the sun. And I shall sit amongst the fruit, bathed in the freshness of new linen, combed and perfumed, and breathing fresh air . . . waiting for you. It shall be just as glorious as the day you were born.

Just after you emerged from my womb, from a liquid to a vaporous world, they took you from me, as the bride is separated from the groom just before the marriage. And in this separation, the bride prepares for a repetition; a new, but old, meeting with her lover. So close were you to me that we were one; but upon birth it is necessary to make preparations to repeat that ancient unity. (How long, long this has taken.) My body was washed, my hair combed of the knots and snarls of thrashing; my bed-linens, damp with a woman's labor and stained with blood, were changed, and my own linens with them. I can still recall the lingering heat and throbbing pains of labor, how weak they made me. But there I sat, propped up with soft pillows, looking flushed, waiting to welcome you to my breast, hoping you would respond to the smells of my body, to the protective heat of it. I have prepared for you today in the very same way and in the same spirit as I did in those earlier days . . . prepared to welcome you.

1834

In a few hours he shall arrive. I am so excited, I can barely keep still. How I anticipate this visit . . . a meeting set freely by him, neither forced nor conjured nor merely wished. This day shall be my birthday — the newest day in my life. All of the days of the past slip away like so many thousands of parched leaves down a stream of spring rain. This is the day which for so long has been due; instead, too many desperate days delayed its coming. During the first days, there was hope; but hope gave way to resignation as each day was but a repetition of the past.

In the days of our past, you had not the least interest in, or desire for me. Although I had never really offered you much that you found desirable, there was, in your growing indifference, a developing element of sternness and moral reproach akin to the silent judgment one feels from the parson. In addition, there was a change in your response to those rare moments when your father and I were mutually involved. When once you would observe us with mild and distant interest, you would now intrude and dissemble our mutuality by leading your father off to handle some highly personal emergency. You even went so far as to engage him in endless discussions which lasted well into the night. Your father would often come to bed exhausted — barely able to unlace his boots. And you also suffered from lack of sleep. That I somehow, was the cause of this suffering worried me so that I set myself to resolve the problem. Doing so surely meant understanding you more than it meant dealing directly with your father. I had somehow to convince you of my good intentions and my innocence.

But how was this to be done, when I was continually compelled to retreat from you lest I unwittingly behave in unacceptable ways? With each encounter, we became ever more distant from one another. Yet this did not soften your critical response; indeed, with each step that I took from you, you took two from me. Many times I wanted to break this fatal pattern, to speak with you alone, to ask you explicitly, to entreat you to understand, to soothe and comfort you as I was sure you needed. But there was such authority in you! I could not help but feel like a child in your presence, continually needing your affection and approval. Whenever I was on the brink of loving you as I yearned to, you came to me disguised as the lover, with standards for the beloved far too high for me to reach. Oh, how I struggled to understand this rejection, this profound hatred! After all this time pondering, I can only guess that your nighttime curiosity became an obsessive interest; that after each nighttime experience, your father's demands on you sharpened the contradiction which you could resolve only by hating me! Your violence would separate your father from me. What terror was in your soul that you failed to keep your father from sin? What more could you do? What more but to plunge still deeper into the promise made by your beloved God, the promise you worked so hard to hear and to trust?

All of those years which you spent in the house of your father. How did I endure them? Was it possible because you went off to school, because you spent so much time with your father and with your God, because you sat for so long with your lessons and your Christian duties? Surely not. In part, I endured them, knowing that I was to blame . . . being what I was; that I deserved to suffer the consequences. But I survived too, believing that someday, you, my son, would come quite by yourself to understand and to forgive me.

That day has come. Blessed be to God!

All that he brought this day was a cross to set by my candle. All that he left this dusk was a candle extinguished by the breath of the living cross that he brought.

Candle spent, it is no longer dusk, but night. The bitterns are gathering over the still South Sea — a mother's womb. Can love flourish in such suffocating blackness? A new flame must appear to keep vigil in the night. It must start a gentle conflagration. Light up the night.

From my window I see a glowing, liquid world. It is a world revealed through the souvenir flames which have lighted the small candle by my bedside. Two worlds have come to light. One beyond my window, one within. They are not spherical worlds, but worlds shaped in floating crosses. The flow of the crosses, urged to movement by the flames, brings them toward me. They tap and caress my cheeks, some from without, some from within, trying I think, to coax me to sleep, to leave the night world where they live alone.

I wonder if it is just the customary restlessness of the past months, or if someone, somewhere, is trying desperately to speak to me, is reaching me only with the very tip of his fluttering voice, now heard from without, now from within. Someone I have always known. I want to whisper into the night air, to ripple the flaming flow: "I am awake. I hear you! We are returning, you and I, to our primal liquid world. I shall be part of you now as you were ever a part of me. The fires of night shall make us equal; they shall authorize our intimacy. The darkness of night shall make of our intimacy a secret of the deep. A secret so gentle, it devours. Curse it for being so gentle; love it for devouring — like you, my son — somewhere on fiery islands, beyond seas I cannot reach from my window."

1836 — 1838

. . . and this possibility pursued him, and he pursued this possibility in his passionate investigation, and this possibility brooded in his silence, and this possibility it was that set in manifold motion the features of his face when he saw a child — and this possibility was that another being owed its life to him.

STAGES ON LIFE'S WAY, *p. 254.*

No one could explain the indescribable sympathy with which he could gaze at a child.

JOURNALS.[16]

Editor's Note to a Prostitute's Will

Much like the first, this, the second set of papers, taxed my resources almost to their limit and demanded far more of me than mere emotional sympathy.

These papers were wrapped in an oilskin envelope[17] which appeared to be self-sealed. The slithery, semi-porous surface of the oilskin compelled touch, as one cannot refrain from touching the skin of a baby. Because it was slightly damp, I concluded that at one time the envelope had been submerged in water and that the rosewood box had been just the sort of vault to preserve the dampness along with its precious contents. The papers within were neatly stacked, and tucked between the pages I found two artificial lilies of the valley,[18] a worn crucifix of gilded tin, and a letter from Berlin. One major effect of the dampness, however, was irreparable damage to the middle pages of the Will. These were spread so densely with water marks, so stained by the dyes of the artificial flowers, so rotted by the rusting cross, that the main body of the Will was just a clump of verbal moss, a jetsam of floating, semi-legible cyphers in various stages of decay.

Here and there, whole sentences were preserved, and these I have used as keys in my effort to break the code. But however much I tried to reduce the code of the middle pages to a single version of a single night, I failed. I was able only to formulate a set of four possible versions.[19] I confess that it is highly unlikely that anyone would compose a Will with four possible versions, a Will subject to such a wide range of interpretation. Yet this particular Will, judging from its rather unorthodox beginning and end, might be expected to be very odd.

The first and last parts of the Will contain information which suggests that the author was a woman of the streets, a prostitute. There is also a clear suggestion that she wrote her Will just prior to committing suicide, and that she intended it to be read, by Kierkegaard, to whom I believe she refers with the term, "Sole Survivor," after her death. Beyond these apparent facts, there are only mysteries. What made the oilskin damp? What was the original message of the middle pages? How did this peculiar document find its way beneath the earth in the company of the other documents in the rosewood box?

Perhaps I am correct in assuming that these questions can be answered by supposing that this woman, the author of the Will, is the prostitute with whom Kierkegaard was involved when he Fell in the year 1836; and that her Will was written in the year 1838 when she surrendered herself to the sea. It was during these two years that SK wrote, "My soul is faint and impotent, in vain I prick the soul of pleasure in her flank, she is exhausted, she rises no more to the royal leap;" that he wrote, "Therefore it is necessary to assume the assistance of God in order to amend oneself." It was in 1837 that SK met Regine Olson; in 1838 that his father died at eighty-two years of age; and it was of the year 1838 that Kierkegaard wrote, "But to God all things are possible. From now on, humanly speaking, I must not only be said to be running into uncertainty, but to be going to certain destruction — and in confidence in God, that is victory. That is how I understood life when I was twelve years old, hence the terrible polemic which filled my soul; that is how I understood it when I was twenty five." These events of significance, having their own peculiar bearing (or lack of it) upon this prostitute's writing, I include for your information — to make of them in interpreting the relationship between her and SK what you will.

Last Will and Testament[21]

Be tolerant, I beg you, of this peculiar document! It is penned by a hand which writes from an errant life. My estate is my body, and that has already been inequitably dispersed over the course of twenty-three years. But, as the adage goes, no woman, not even a married woman, knows how many lovers she has.[22] I resolved some weeks ago to catch up with myself, to become what I have been; or better, to become what I no longer am. My existence has become vestigial, de trop, and my child continually makes the mistake of taking my mere appearance for reality. My child! No. My child will not become a "Sole Survivor." My child shall not succeed me at all; not because I shall not exist, but because I have never existed. To succeed me is inevitably to become a miserable failure, like every other accursed child who has only a leather-breasted mother, like every child who must be sent thirsting for milk into the polluted water coursing sluggishly through the gutters of Christianshavn. On this theme alone do I speak with authority. To withhold a child's inheritance is, for some, to impoverish it. To deny my child its heritage is the singular path open to me if the child is to be the child of a mother — if I am to be the mother of the child.

So, my child, you shall have your second birth in these pages; and the birth shall be a delivery more glorious than the birth before. You shall be born in this, my absolute renunciation of responsibility for you! In later years do not imagine that I sat here at this bedside table projecting romantic scenes for which I am saving you. In my imagination there are no images of future sunny days in carriage rides over the bridge to the excitements of Copenhagen; there are no images of a small form daydreaming in the soft grass or in troughs of clear lakes; there are no tales of holidays spent with the pure sounds of laughter, in leaping legs disturbing the silent snows. No images left; no spirit for imagining. I have done with imagination, a despicable faculty. Who needs this all-too-human faculty with its promise of hope? With a cold objectivity I am certain that whatever shall become of you will be a whole life better, my child, than were I to hang on. It is by no means, my beloved, that I trust the world to save you. I speak from the utter impotence of my intentions mirrored in the infinite void which once was my imagination.

"Farewell," then.

And now to you, my Sole Survivor, I have a last bequest. With palms upturned I stand before exploding suns, the pieces of lint in my otherwise empty, turned-out pockets waiting to be picked clean. Here they are, piece by piece, the remnants, the fragments of my life; your precious facts, your long-sought information . . . such as it is.

I understand that you have, these past two years, been a constant visitor to the House, pursuing its pathetic inhabitants with your obsessive questions concerning my

whereabouts, so that you might find help in piecing together the events of that night . . . that infamous night . . .
your thorn in the flesh![23] They write me of their annoy-
ance at your dogged persistence and their repulsive pity for
you. They beg me to come out of concealment, to take
you off their hands, to satisfy your craving for information. Do you howl like a weakened wolf with an empty
stomach? How comforting it was to imagine that this hunger made you, over two years, as desperate as I became in
one night! But now, as I have dispensed with imagination —
and with it the whole filthy realm of hope and possibility
for reasons which will become apparent in due course — I
no longer enjoy or benefit from your despair. If I cannot
fill my pockets with small gifts, neither do I want to line
them with lint. I want only to go out if not pure, then
CLEAN. So do not fashion yourself trustworthy; and do
not imagine that my speech is a gift to you. It is merely a
bequest to one I have designated "MY SOLE SURVIVOR"
. . .indeed, a questionable social status! If you can at all be
called trustworthy, it is as a criminal who survives only as
he keeps secrets. If you receive undeserved fortune, it is as
the child in the fairy tale who is duped into an oven by the
witch's gingerbread house.

How many pockets must I empty? How many holes
must I unplug before the void emerges? Allow me to begin
. . . or, as the case may be, to end . . .

I

The stage I set for you was real; it was precisely as you ordered. The room was utterly black, only the moonshine of

white sheets faintly illumining the old wooden cross you
sent that morning, with instructions that it be set by the
bed upon a small table. It is a disturbing cross with a
family insignia burned out in black. In contrast to the upstairs darkness, the downstairs is ablaze with countless candles shining forth in as many heated crosses. And there is
music, too. An ambulant musician is playing on a reed
pipe. I cannot say for certain what, since he is in the next
courtyard.[24] It is the song of Dionysios, untroubled by the
Apollonian lights. A nuptial opera. Yes! The entire crowd
is a wedding party; but the wedding has already taken
place . . . they are too late . . . but no matter. Their cele-
brations will never be more than anticipatory. The bridegroom is bringing the bride to this place which, although
dark, is not at all magical or strange, but absolutely familiar. One might even call it home were it not that when
night falls, all space becomes alien.

It is late at night when we arrive by carriage at our
well-ordered house, from a journey of four nights to nowhere. You persuade me down the precarious heights of
the carriage steps with the objectivity of a footman.[25]
With the lightest of steps we approach our temple. You
start almost instinctively toward the glare of the downstairs chamber, and lift one candle from the entranceway.
But I lead you up a back staircase which trails like a kite-
tail from our dark destination. All this time you avert
your eyes, but you are not anxious. Your arm rests upon
mine like the touch of my own shadow upon the edges of
my body. And we climb, God knows, through the stages
of night, the densest of all mountains. After some minutes,
you turn suddenly and interrupt our ascent with speech.
You ask me, in absolutely pure tones, to lead you through

the Valley of the Shadow of Death, beyond your fear of
evil. And with these words, for the first time, I become
aware of my mission and marvel at my ability to hold my
tongue . . . so quietly and resolutely had I undertaken your
task. All was in silent readiness, and no word needed uttering. But you spoke. And the trust of your speech ignited
my longing. Your submissiveness evoked my responsibility.

But of course you expected more — or should I say less
— of me, your hired temptress!! You contracted, you
thought, with one trained in keeping a bargain, in obedience to the letter of the law! You gave not a thought to
the possibility that I should succumb to so simple a dis-
traction, to so minor a temptation as speech. You fool!
You lacked the humanity to imagine the agonizing years
of waiting, of longing to hear your words. Silence? No! I
am unable to conceal from you whither this course leads.[26]
When your words bespeak your trust, I interrupt the pilgrimage on some convenient landing and sweep you up to
me so that the whole of your body touches the whole of
my own. And I bend your head across my shoulder in a
benediction.[27] And then I say what I have for so long
needed to say. So sweetly do the words emerge from my
lips, I can taste them . . . those words which had lingered
with an eternal patience in my throat, waiting to be
spoken.

Will it ever be possible for you to conceive my horror
at your response? Pushing those words down my throat
with such force as to send me choking to the wall. What
was it that you could not, would not understand as you
fell to your knees in confusion and protestation, insisting
upon our original bargain? Surely you remember how,
rising to your feet, you cast me up the stairs by my skirts,

imploring me ever upward with words which have long
echoed through these halls. Even were the dark mountain
of those steps the path to Purgatory, I should have chased
myself up it long after you had lost your voice. But, alas!
At the top of the stairs I am caught by the rosewood box
which hangs, filled with small change, upon the door; the
box whose elaborate carving presses painfully into my
back. Caught at the Devil's last frontier. There, violence
and hatred course through my body like a demonic stream
of fire, transforming it into a molten whirlpool from which
I cannot return. The coolness of our shadow play, and
with it the legality of your precious contract, is burned to
ashes.

My fire is life. Try as you do to resist me with the passivity of ritual, then of consciousness, and then of uncon-
sciousness, you cannot. This night you are already sparked
by dark desire. To coax you willingly, by the most wanton
seduction, across the threshold from cold light into the
flaming night was my demonic revenge. Yes. I am Satan's
daughter.

But how could I have anticipated you! My stiff, formal,
wholly objective man, surpassing even me in the demonism
of the flesh! The likes of me are usually prepared for such
reserved types; but you were, frankly, unmanageable. You
wished to feel all the gates of sin open within your own
breast, the whole kingdom of incalculable demonic possibilities. Everything would not be sufficient.[28] Though
your hopes were certain to be disappointed, I could but
respond, and then respond ten times over again. As the
fisherman and the big fish love their struggle, I, too, loved
every phase of the war. But I hated every phase of the love
making. I hated it! But you must have hated beyond me.

It must have been at the very point where love and hate collided, where passion turned to violence, that you seized the candle and set the cross on fire.[29]

It was because of the fire that I was released from my job, and ultimately, from all jobs. In one night I had achieved a reputation. The event was of historic interest — to say nothing of the salacious curiosity amongst my colleagues. However, fires are just too risky for most Houses. My silence has, at least, preserved my memory in conversations of the curious. It is still our secret that the climactic moments of our lust, the moments of supreme human power, were consummated not in floods of human passion, but instead in the fires of Hell set by your cold, abstract hand igniting that old wooden cross.

When a woman comes ready to bear child, she comes to the bed chamber in her purest linens. It would be a shame that she should appear the same when her husband cannot have her. So her husband believes her, that her linens are for him, a sign of sweeter love. But he knows, too, that the love is more inclusive. And to her glance which is more loving and tender than ever, he responds. Happy the woman who has no need of more dreadful expedients for bearing a child.[30]

II

Your letter came with a proposal — to set a stage. How grand! Does not courtship require a stage setting? How sweet, when the prospective bride prepares for her bridegroom in her finest lace, revealing in its intricacy the curves of her body just beyond his touch. See her hands resting lightly curled in her lap, waiting for him to beckon; see her head bent at an illusory angle; hear her words like faint scents of perfume capturing his attention and intoxicating him.

What of the wedding itself! How grand the stage setting then! To me even the opera is no rival to its glory. Look! The young girl in the flowing snows of the wedding gown, with wildflowers gushing in warm streams through its winter; witness how it is sanctified by the enclosing stained glass, with the black of her parson and her bridegroom, supporting her white. Gaze upon the household of millions[31] massed to witness by applause. The eyes feast upon the solemn ballet — the march down the aisle, the pirouettes of the bridal pair, the arched movements of the parson's cupped hands encircling bowed heads. And to the ears, the deep strains of an old organ whose rich, almost dissonant overtones bespeak its great history of service to this age-old drama. A proposal for a stage setting; a courtship; a wedding!

The house was lighted by hundreds of candles blazing out in as many heated crosses. The old reed organ was playing the minuet from Mozart's Don Giovanni — our wedding song, you called it. The crowd downstairs is boisterous, in celebration of they knew not what. But no matter. The scene is exactly as you require. Our upstairs room is ready. It is utterly black except for the moonshine of white sheets illumined by the candle at the foot of your wooden cross, which I placed that morning upon a small bedside table. To the sound of an old organ, the bridegroom is bringing his bride to this place. The place was once an opera house, but now it is absolutely familiar. One might even call it home except that when the curtain falls, all space becomes theatrical.

For four hours we ride by carriage to the country. Hardly a word is spoken but for the gestures of courtship. (Wasn't it really a monologue? Or was it a dialogue with a mythical hero? No matter.) It is late at night when we arrive. You persuade me down the carriage steps with the objectivity of a footman. I start, almost instinctively, toward the magic theatre downstairs, to be applauded to encores by our audience. But you remember the back staircase which joins us directly to our dark destination. I lift up my eyes and see afar off the dark door;[32] but my glance turns longingly to you. Silently you avert your face and silently we begin our ascent. Up, up through the stages of our stage. Silently. Fearlessly. I, floating upon my own yearning, on the wings of my girlish fantasies. Were this dark mountain endless, I should have had eternal patience equal to it; my life has hammered my soul into nothing if not patience. Too soon our ascent is terminated by the touch of the rosewood box on the door of this, our honeymoon chamber. By this time I am filled to overflowing with the sweet intensity of human passion; it courses through and pervades my body, though my lace remains unruffled, my fingers limp, my breathing soft. Only the scent of my perfume seems to intensify. Still, we say not a word.

I wonder now what the story really was. No matter. I shall never know. I leave the rest of this drama to be told and re-told, not in the sordid breaths of a dying beast, but in the breathlessness of a flushed new woman whispering to her earless, full-breasted mother.

In our rather ordinary drama, you never once gaze

upon me with the sympathy due a virgin about to surrender to human love. Your eyes are passive and your very
existence seems held in my glance. As I am about to turn
you toward me, you disappear from beneath my fingers
into the dark room. After a brief, anxious moment, I hear
your voice from a distance. And before I understand the
words, I hear only their sound echoing from the vicinity of
my bed. I look. There you are; stretched over it, illumined
in vague, quivering spots by the candle alongside. The reflection of the cross is flung between your hips, your arms
outstretched as if in a second reflection. A corpse; half-
dead; oozing the warmth of the living in ghostly tones.
You beckon me to you — a beckoning which was meant to
precede words — and ask to be stripped and consumed.
Stripped and consumed!

Flash! I see a sign in a butcher's shop beneath the
freshly killed fowl: "Stripped and Consumed — Satisfaction Guaranteed."

Flash! I imagine a back room in which nests of plump
ladies with filthy aprons and sterilized fingers are undressing, feather by feather, those wholly satisfactory birds.

Flash! They toss them into neat positions upon the
sawdust to meet a starving public. Yes. There you are —
flung across my bed this night.

With so few words, a trivial alteration of plot, the
play changes. The hush of the honeymoon chamber becomes the sterile silence of the plucking room, where the
plump ladies remain concealed except for their adroit fingers pluck, pluck, plucking their birds. Pluck! The over-
coat. Pluck! The jacket. Pluck! Pluck! Boots and stockings.
Pluck, pluck! Trousers. Pluck, pluck, pluck, pluck, button,
button, button, button, and all the buttons thereof.

But wait! What have we! One of the birds is responding! As I, in the silence of newly falling snow, achieve my goal: an absolutely plucked, clean, featherless carcass, the bird revives in protest! It flaps its bony transparent wings and crows in indiscriminate sounds as if trying to establish its individuality! Indeed, one would think this bird was human, insulted by the supposition that it is just another bird, born and raised for the sole purpose of being stripped and consumed. The bird has lost its wits! Look! It seems to be turning upon itself now. It has become just a mass of limp appendages beating randomly against themselves; and quickly exhausted by its own impotence, it lunges, half-expired to the ground, leaving behind clouds of dancing sawdust.

That sawdust, turned to ashes, was all that was left that night after the upstairs fire. Who would have thought that such an insignificant candle, knocked over onto a wooden cross in the insipid rage of a plucked fowl, could have created such a blaze? And though not a soul should believe me, there is hardly another explanation for it. But, of course, even were my story credible, my so-called career would still have ended.

When the girl becomes the woman, and craves motherhood, she virginally hides her body so that her husband has no more a mistress but a wife. And the husband and the wife become to each other no longer as one, but as multiple. And in that multiplicity a child is born. Happy the child who is not in another way born of a mother.[33]

III

Your proposal arrived, it seemed, as a call to accounting,

my day of reckoning, when I should have to make my confession in the macrocosmic arms of one man. So, I was finally being sent a man who would save me. And I was to construct the altar upon which my confession and baptism were to take place. I did not quite understand all the symbolism; nor did I really try. To me, this was the call of Fate, when one is required simply, unquestionably, to obey. This, my Fate, was to be lifted forever out of bondage to the night life of Christianshavn. To this Fate I was prepared to surrender myself wholly.

So I set the stage, transforming my shabby but efficient stable into a divine manger. As if heralding my salvation in anticipation, the downstairs is white with countless candles blazing out in so many fiery crosses. An ambulant musician in the next courtyard is playing the minuet from Mozart's Don Giovanni, beckoning the confessant forward in the recognizable tones of a reed-pipe. The crowd downstairs is jubilant; choruses of human angels celebrating in advance the salvation of another soul.

Upstairs, all is ready. My oil lamps are removed and replaced by one candle shining upwards upon the wooden crucifix sent by your messenger, replacing my own cross which is made not of wood, but of tin gilded around the edges. The crucifix is placed, as you ordered, on a small table beside the bed. The bedding is changed to new linen. To this new place you shall escort me, your confessant; a place, once a witch's pot, now a sanctified altar. One might even call it home except that when the spells of night are cast, all space becomes bewitched.

For four hours we ride by carriage to the country. During this journey I speak about my past. You listen to my melancholy account: that I was born into a theatrical family, a regular circus of characters; out of the womb of a brilliant and wealthy but wholly dissolute mother, who spent her life being saved for history and from guilt by some five or six or maybe even seven missionaries to this singular cause — zealots who identified history with the public alleys of Christianshavn and guilt with the treasurer's indebtedness. Mother had little she called her own, little she seemed to want; except perhaps a pair of silk stockings which continually trailed in folds down her legs, but which, at moments of critical social importance, like meeting family and old friends, she lifted up sharply by their edges, straightening the wrinkles to a smooth respectability. I, too, was her symbol of respectability, ignored for the most part, only remembered and displayed when social custom required a family. The old lady wound up on a farm plucking chickens; while I, paradoxically enough, was sent to the city. She had little use for silk in the wiry coops; but I was left longing for a real family.

You listen while I recount my searches in Copenhagen for a family to which I could belong. You listen to my adventures wandering in and out of various groups; families of singularly unconventional varieties: families of vagrants, families of illiterates, families of traitors, families of nomads, families of aberrants, families of failures — all; and I the adopted daughter of them all. Until, reading the newspaper ads one grey morning, I happened upon a "Help Wanted" placed by a familiar name, one I immediately recognized as belonging to a distant relative who was the object of envy in many a family conversation.[34] But as I am about to speak of my position as a servant in the house of this wealthy relative, and of my initiation into the rather unwholesome duties which accompanied the job, you urge the horses forward at great speed, till the carriage comes, via their death-defying leaps, to our appointed destination.

You are as breathless as the horses; and I — in the midst of bringing my sordid past back to life, a past ready to be purged — I think to myself that whatever else needs saying must now be said in a more private place. So I allow you to persuade me down the carriage steps, to guide me to the place where I am to complete my confession. We bypass the crowd downstairs, knowing that the time has not yet come for real jubilation, but we pause for a moment, sensing the quality of it, anticipating the joy with the crowd — but in silence. We begin our ascent with measured steps, each step confirming the seriousness of our purpose, each step responding to the ground beneath it, and feeling, too, the loss of ground as we strain and reach one higher. We cannot, we must not look back; for as we climb, we leave a void behind us. We are climbing, and so long as we do not falter the void supports us and our commitment to the summit. We look not at each other but ahead and upward. We are two forms: I too much a body; you, my shadow, lighter than air, leading me through the stages of the night, the densest of all mountains.

This is the dark mountain upon which I, for so long, have wandered aimlessly. Often I trod my lonely way, but I found no rest.[35] I could not comprehend that it was a mistake to believe I could accomplish the task alone. I could not understand why I might not be forgiven, why I could not seize control of my own fate. In great desperation and impotence, I would throw myself upon my face. Alone on my mountain, I would pray to be delivered. But Echo alone would respond in the sterile tones of my all-too-familiar voice reverberating in stone. O rootless, tree-less mountain upon which no solitary human can gain a foothold! Now, now I shall make my ascent. Now your smooth slopes angle out in steps made for human feet. Now there is a guide who knows the way . . . who makes the way. Cursed mountain . . . you must — you MUST — love me. (So I believed!)

As we walk pensively along our way, I think of my mother, and of all the false prophets, the imitation saviors who drove her out into the wilderness. I see her image projected in a spot of light before me. There in the enclosing darkness she sits, a smooth-as-leather-bodied old woman with a worn-out soul escaping in folds down her legs. She rises to tend the chickens, still with a puzzled look on her face. Why does she still feel lost after having searched for so long? Why is she tired even though she is at rest? Why the persistent sense of guilt even after having given so much away? This is her Fate; but it is not to be mine. I am to be saved! To come home, clean and at peace! I have been granted what has been withheld from her.

We reach the door to the altar with its rosewood box now almost a holy relic, not to the sound of trumpets but to the delicate tones of a reed-pipe playing the minuet from Mozart's Don Giovanni; not to the blaze of heavenly light but to the graceful flame of a simple candle illumining a wooden cross. I do not move for fear that I shall break the tenuous silence of this awesome night, that some clumsy shift of my body will precipitate an explosion of suns. I stand in place. Waiting. Watching you. Relying, as an obedient servant, upon your powers and your mastery. You move to my bed, and for some long suspenseful moments there is the burden of patience shared somehow

mutually; until you speak, beckoning me in a whisper:
"Seduce me!"

My body tenses into a single knot. I whisper back to
myself that this is Temptation calling me again; but this
time the call is explicit; this time there is the promise of
redemption should I marshall the power to resist. This man
was sent to try my will (what there is left of it) one last
time. The only time left. He is testing me, and I shall win.
I shall show him that I am truly ready. So, my inner monologue progresses, each phrase shoring up my will, each
sentence steeling my resolve to stand fast, to hold tight. I
shall talk to myself forever, if necessary, to prove my
readiness.

How do you interpret my silence, my absolute reserve?
You are embarrassed! My passivity dramatizes your ignorance, your naiveté. You have no conception whatever of
what you want, why you are here! You picked up your
clues from cheap novels and cheaper rumors. You had only
some shopworn daydreams which you hoped would magically become facts. But when all the daydreams crumble
into bits of broken glass, and me with them, all you can do
is ask for
"Help!"

HELP is what you called. But I still misunderstood
you! What a fool I was! I believed you were offering; not
begging. And I began to weep as I can only remember
weeping once, when I believed my mother was coming
back to me. It was a weeping preliminary to the rainbow,
the torrential prelude to the cleansing of earths. Soon I
hear you entering dissonantly into my tearful fugue. You
are weeping, too. You are weeping, too. You are weeping.
Weeping, weeping. And all my tears rejoin all the blood in

my body; and all of it, in all the desperate harmony of one tidal wave, crashes out of my edgeless body.

This is a ceremony. We are its celebrants. It is a ceremony of baptism taking place upon a baptismal altar. But now it is clear that yours is the soul which is called forward, not mine. Yours is the soul whose Fate is at stake, not mine. This is your initiation, and I am hired to celebrate the service. So. Bloodless and tearless, I approach the altar. I take your head in my ice-cold, transparent hands, and I wipe away your tears. With trembling body, you kneel at my feet in readiness; waiting. Up, then. This is no time for delay. The procedures take over from here. I am merely their instrument, their bodily agent. Would that the choruses downstairs could see us! What would they see?

They would witness the baptism of a child into manhood. Around here, nothing unusual. The child is nervous, afraid; his body is all too deliberately responsive, far too focused, wanting too desperately to perform these rites of passage. He strains too much; he is too excited, too intent. Poor child! But I can only administer the rites, only raise the knife. The lamb must be relaxed, positively lost in my gesture, intoxicated with the sparkle of the blade. Impotent child! You are not yet ready to receive the blessing, to wet my blade with your blood; for to be ready is also to be quite casual, almost disdainful of the event. No. It has never worked this way.

The service has terminated; it has not been completed. It is over; but it has not ended. It is gone; but it never was. I have tried to carry it through. Perhaps the shift in the ceremony was too much, my strength sapped from it. With my mother's face I lie upon the bed. You forget me in reflexive sighs and mutterings on its edge. Your face is buried in your palms, and you coat them continually with tears. You weep and weep and weep; and your weeping grows more intense as it seems the answer to some increasingly melancholy commentary you silently recite to yourself.

Had I another face than the face of my mother, I should have tried to comfort you. But you can understand now why I did not. Like an infant, you became quite hysterical. You threw yourself upon the cross with a sigh that achieved voice, a sigh which caught fire, the fire which, in its own peculiar Fatefulness, ended my questionable career.

When the woman becomes old and is still without child, the husband, too, is not without sorrow at the thought that he and his wife are separated more and more, that the woman who first lay under his heart and later reposed upon it will be so near to him no more. So they mourn together for the brief period of mourning; and then, in the many forms of rebirth, they mourn no more. Happy the woman who has kept her man as near and needed not to sorrow anymore.[36]

IV

I received your letter with its proposal, as automatically as I had received proposals in the past except that the explicitness of the request set me to wondering. Most men admit no such clear and detailed ideas of their desires. What they hope for usually becomes clear in process. Commonly, the evening begins in an ordinary manner, suddenly shifting to the perverse at some critical point in this pattern. Like the time I was summoned to the house of an enormously fat gentleman who, after an elaborate ritual of undressing, at the moment just prior to the touch of his naked body to mine, insisted upon feeding me inordinate amounts of gourmet delicacies, followed by a final, consummating jug of wine, poured down my throat by his trembling hands. He was, paradoxically enough, typical. But you insisted on a precise set of conditions. In an apparently calm, deliberate letter, you described the scene: a dark room upstairs, a freshly made bed, a wooden cross upon a small bedside table, illumined by a candle, and a reed-pipe in the next courtyard playing the minuet from Don Giovanni! So, that morning I set about transforming the place according to your description.

Whereas most of my previous involvements with the unorthodox needs of men (and women) occurred too spontaneously for deliberation, these very explicit paragraphs detailing well-organized preparations gave me too much time for thought. As I was removing the ornaments from my room (my souvenirs of artificial flowers, tiny metallic trinkets, picture postcards from around the world), I felt as if I were uncovering some awful, hidden reality which lay buried somewhere behind the walls or beneath the floor boards; as if I were tampering with the face of the room, and something monstrous was about to emerge. When I had almost stripped the room bare, I took a good, hard look at it.

For the first time, I saw where I was, what I was calling "home." There was only one word for it — *shabby.* "Shabby," I thought first with scientific scrutiny; and then, "shabby," in moral reproach. I had never really seen the place in daylight. The sun revealed a multiplicity of relatively clean rectangles upon the wall, their edges emerging from the dust which had gathered around my pictures. Interspersed among these were various-sized hooks and nails jutting out like so many small invitations to a hanging. The imitation-lace doilies, now removed from bureaus, revealed elaborate patterns of cigar burns, wine glass rings, and wet coins. The slow rust of stained wallpaper linked the window curtains, yellow with the grime of years, to the jaundiced air of Christianshavn (a town sick too long to arouse concern). The room leered out at me! Only the carved rosewood box upon the door looked respectable; it reflected a finer life which this house may have enjoyed in days prior to its use as a palace of corruption. And too, a sketch of my mother, a departing gift from some one of her undiscovered artist-saviors, looking too much like a madonna, seemed not to share in the shabbiness of its environment.

I must have stood for some time, lost in the atmosphere, lost in the memories of how these things in this room, now old and familiar, were when new. How had the life in this room been lost to me? Obviously, its life had become its own, and I had only now become aware of it — a life in which I, too, had lived, and one which also included the one-dimensional lives of many men, some women. We all lived the life of the room — I and my whole amorphous family. How had I failed to be aware of this truth? I must have dropped so far into the night life of Christianshavn that my realities had become my waking dreams.

Standing there, confronting my shabby world as an observer, I was shocked to find how it contradicted my dreams. I only dreamed that my room was the backstage room of some famous actress; or the estate room of some international celebrity; or the hidden attic room in some Spanish castle. Any room at all — except the room in which I really lived! This room! Crashing in on me.

The barrenness of the room, its ugly truths, sobered me considerably that morning, and I went about my complicated preparations self-consciously as if I were a new arrival in this world, marvelling at everything for the first time. Yet, completing the preparations toward early evening, I began to feel a renewed familiarity with the place. I might even have decided it was home, except that when the sun sets, all worlds become alien planets.

The stage you made me set during that unsettling day was so artificial that the stark reality of my life was a sudden shock. Strangely enough, I was anxious to discover what was to happen that evening, that toward which all these preparations were directed — not as an anticipation of a novel event, but as a first clear awareness of a wholly ordinary one. "Let us see," I said to myself, "what I really have been up to in this room." I was genuinely and seriously curious about this lost self of mine and the life it lived here. It was about time that I got to know the sort of girl who lived in this miserable place.

All of the props are in their places, each one a reminder, a signpost for consciousness: the noisy crowd downstairs, the minuet from Don Giovanni, the dark, bare room, the fresh linens, the bedside table, the small candle, and the wooden cross. These are all in their appointed places when we arrive by carriage from a four-hour ride to the country.

We ride together in harmony. Our talk is quiet and calm, talk floating in and out of focus. I listen to the words and watch the gestures. They appear quite harmless, really; words and gestures made by ordinary people even to the fact that we remain strangers. The silences which fall throughout our dialogue carry the slight uneasiness of strangers in a social situation, except that I sense you are lost in the silence. When I resume speaking, your attention is given in the surprise of waking from a sleep. But I assume that you, as I, have something on your mind, perhaps something related to this special night.

We dismount the carriage, you helping me down with the objectivity of a footman. The house rises from the cobblestones, a strangely alive presence in this dull, drowsy-with-fog street. The moon is hidden and the candles from the downstairs windows are the only lights visible in the night. They cast a glow upon the heavy fog which manages to descend only half way down the house. The upper half of the house (and along with it, the whole town) is utterly black, blotting out whatever flicker of light might be shining from the small candle by the cross.

> O pale moon!
> Thou that dividest the seasons here on earth,
> Why art thou then so strait towards me, thou cold,
> Thou sallow miser? Why art thou so mean?[37]

I know this house. I recognize it. But it is a house I also do not know — a haunted house — and my heart flutters for an instant as we approach the entrance. To the left of the downstairs living quarters is a hidden, rarely used staircase rejected by most in favor of the one which gives access to the upstairs rooms through the downstairs parlors. It is arranged that we use this less-traveled way. Since this staircase is silent and dark, senses other than sight and hearing must aid those who would climb it. The stairway smells as a winding sewer receiving waste from the parlors. The scents of human bodies are so intense that I am sure we are about to trip over some, sprawled across the steps. These are not smells from a strictly human world but are more like smells from the sea — smells of seaweed freshly thrown up upon the shore, smells of jellyfish caught between rusting mussel shells and driftwood. Yes. The smells of a human sandpit by the sea! I feel that I am descending into the sea: 50 fathoms, 75 fathoms, 100 fathoms, 200 fathoms, 70,000 fathoms.[38]

The water pressure increases; my lungs grow heavy within me; my breathing becomes strained and audible. I am sinking, irretrievably lost. Just as I am about to scream to relieve the pressure, I reach out and my hand touches the cool surface of the rosewood box. At once, as if entering a vacuum, the pressures of the sea subside. My relief impels me toward my bed, and I allow it to comfort me, as if I had been swimming a very long distance and was near to exhaustion.

Only after some minutes of rest do I catch sight of your impatient face beside mine. As I begin to move, I feel my skirts clinging to my legs; whisps of hair on my neck drip, and a stream of liquid trickles down my back. I have been to sea! I am dripping wet! As I try to wipe my brow, the drops spill over my lashes into my eyes. Your image changes through this watery veil. I cannot make you out quite clearly enough. Who are you? I shake my head like a cat in from a rainstorm. I rub my eyes, but I cannot seem to dry off. You could be anyone — Hans, Alan, Michael, Peter, Lars . . . anyone! I pull you down toward me, pulling your face to my eyes so as to clarify your image, to see who you really are. But before my focus sharpens you kiss my lips and throw yourself upon me. For some minutes we struggle at cross purposes. It is the struggle of love making and the struggle of war; it is the struggle into intoxication and the struggle to consciousness.

I lose in the physical struggle because I am already weakened by my descent, pulled down by the tides of my dripping skirts. But in the achievement of consciousness I have won, and I understand that I am hired to surrender. Suddenly, my body goes limp with its wet shroud, and I lose myself in response to you, the source of my revelation. Yet I am watchful. The struggles of your body dominate me, pulling mine along with them, continually threatening my attempts to preserve consciousness. But I win. I understand, finally, what is happening. With each phase of the struggle, while you become wetter, I dry off. My vision is no longer clouded; my mouth, in fact, is parched; my body turns to sand and salt. You can only wash up upon it, wave after wave. But with it your body shall never merge.

I, of all people, certainly understand your rage. You are entitled to it! I understand what impels you to tear the candle from beneath the wooden cross. I understand why you brandish it before my sun-bleached face; I understand why you make threats to disfigure me. I understand. For when I look upon the candle flame, and through it into your eyes, I see my image reflected there; I see my face — a clenched fist, and I know what I look like, what I really am. I am the daughter of my mother! So go on, say I, make my appearance coincidental with my reality. Set the sand afire!

I am told that the blaze went undiscovered for some time — enough time to have destroyed most of the upstairs quarters, but also just enough time to permit a rescue. They tell me but that for the damp clothes in which together they were wrapped, our two bodies would surely have perished. So praise the gods who saved us, those gods who thereby enabled . . . well, whatever they enabled.

When the wife is big with child and the husband must keep distance, the woman has a deeper intimacy in readiness within her, lest her man disappear in the distance. In the intimacy of the family, the man is held. Happy is the child who is born into such intimacy.[39]

As are my riches, such is my bequest. Amen. You have it all, dear Sole Survivor. And what benefactor could deny the very gifts for which he had hoped? What benefactor could wish to reduce the extent of this estate? Try though he foolishly might to do so — to simplify it, to apportion it, to sell it, or to give it away; even with quick, nimble fingers, to hide it in some bottom drawer, he will be relentlessly haunted by its presence. For pieces of lint, my dear, those worthless, detestable, fragments, have a way of sticking around. I, alone, shall depart, leaving these scraps in my place.

Before I leave this room, I shall gaze once more out of my window into the streets of Christianshavn. It will be raining. And the rain will fall very deliberately; but yet as if it wanted to slip to earth unnoticed, so it will hesitate briefly before sounding its call upon the cobblestones. In this spirit of soft silence, the rain will guide me to the sea.

With an oilskin protecting my documents, I shall leave this room to join the rain. As I cross the threshold, I shall notice the carved rosewood box which hangs empty upon the open door. It shall loom large and outstanding as if offering itself, imploring me not to abandon it. In sympathy I shall remove it and place my oilskin envelope inside. With this my only baggage, I shall, without looking back, be up and off to Gilbjerg.[40] I shall take the road from the inn through Sortebro, across the barren tract that runs along the seacoast, one mile and a quarter to the north, to the highest point in the district. There I shall stand in the dark silence of this night, pressing the textured edges of the rosewood box to my breast, listening to the sea striking up its profoundly calm song of welcome to the oncoming dawn. I shall see no sail on the vast waters, only the mutual bounding of sea and heaven. While on the other side, the busy noise of life shall stand in readiness, waiting for the patient fog, which now smothers it, to lift. The birds will proclaim their premature morning. And I shall be already awake, at the edge of the sea. So close to home shall I be.

And the many who claimed to love me shall come forth, decked out in festival costumes, from their sea-graves; or rather it shall seem to me as if they had not died, but were frozen in the pale silence of patience, waiting for me, their wayward daughter, shipwrecked upon land. I shall feel so content in their midst, their amorphous images spilling wave upon gentle wave over me in so many liquid embraces. I shall be, as it were, out of the body, lured spellbound into their water world. Perhaps I shall toss my baggage in as an offering, and as a prelude. Perhaps, briefly, I shall hear the hoarse screech of the gulls and see in the distance the gathering of the stormy petrels, reminding me that I stand as a fragment, alone and forsaken, blessed by no such communal bond, nor with voice to pierce the heavens; reminding me that I am but a sparrow[41] who has fallen voicelessly to the cold earth. My destiny is not to be lifted heavenward; nor is my home upon the sand. I shall never ascend, but fall repeatedly to the shore, with wings weakened repeatedly and cracked by the pressures of the upper world in its eternal struggle with the pull of the earth below. To the eyes of those who walk upon earth, and to those of the gods, I shall appear lifeless, flung there just at the edge of the sea. The irregular pulsations of a tiny heart will be the only invisible signs of life. No help from heaven or from earth shall come, and I shall be unable to do anything but listen, to hear voices calling me in the dips and soft foamings of waves, in the lightness of the morning dew, in the sweet taste of fresh raindrops, beckoning me in, tempting me, teasing me, touching me, licking me, moving me, lifting me, wafting me up, up, and up and higher, and again deeper, again and again, and oh, how buoyantly, and finally, ah, away, away home.

1837 — 1847

Only his children Job did not receive again double, because a human life is not a thing that can be duplicated.

REPETITION, *p. 26.*

Editor's Note to Regine's Tale

This, the third set of papers, was a pleasure to behold, its contents stacked page upon perfect page in a dark envelope sealed with a faint coat of arms, which might well have been used for official business by some municipal government.[42] These pages contained the most highly polished, orderly, consistent prose of any of the documents. I had little to do but to reduplicate them. There was but one problem. The title page made reference to a two-part story. Yet all that appeared beneath it was one part numbered "Two." Part "One" was missing!

Since the dedication was signed "Regine," I have assumed that the entire work was written by Regine Olson, Kierkegaard's true love, and that it was conceived and offered by her as a birthday gift to SK, dated May 5, 1847, which would have been Kierkegaard's thirty-fourth birthday. It seems reasonable to assume that part Two was written sometime around 1847; and there is a clear suggestion that it is a long-delayed conclusion to a Part One which was written well before that year. Perhaps it was written during the very first year of their courtship when it was Kierkegaard's habit to bring Regine certain books and, by studying these with her, to teach her something, indirectly, of his extraordinary nature.[43]

Anyone reading Part Two discovers immediately its

basis in the tale of Alaeddin and the Wonderful Lamp, a tale in which SK had a continuing interest. This explicit duplication of the story of Alaeddin provided me, as an interpreter, with the basis I needed to reconstruct Part One. By taking very careful account of both the obvious and the subtle changes made by Regine. I was able to pick up the loose threads with which her middle part began and to reweave from the traditional story what must have been her beginning, so that the piece became a whole of two parts.

By including Part One which is, for the most part, my contribution to the old story, I am compelled to refer the entire manuscript to the years 1837, when SK first met Regine, and 1847, when Regine married F. Schlegel and wrote Part Two. In 1840, Kierkegaard journeyed to his ancestral home in Jutland; in 1840, he proposed to Regine; in 1841, he broke his engagement and left for Berlin with the words, "You say: she was beautiful. Oh what do you know about it; I know it, for her beauty cost me tears — I myself brought flowers with which to adorn her. I would have hung all the ornaments of the world upon her . . . and as she stood there in all her array — I had to go — as her joyful look, so full of life, met mine — I had to go — and I went out and wept bitterly." It was in 1843 that Regine became engaged to F. Schlegel; in 1846, that SK considered qualifying himself for ordination; and in 1847 that Regine married Schlegel. In 1847, SK wrote, "But to God all things are possible. From now on, humanly speaking, I must not only be said to be going into uncertainty, but to be going to certain destruction — and, in confidence in God, that is victory. That is how I understood life when I was ten years old, hence the terrible polemic which filled my soul; that is how I understood it when I was twenty-five, and now that I am thirty-four. That is why Paul Moller called me the most completely polemical of men." The events of significance which occurred in these ten years, having their own peculiar bearing (or lack of it) upon Regine's writing, I include for your information — to make of them in interpreting her relationship to SK what you will.

SK:

Let this account serve not merely to return a story for a story, nor merely to continue the tradition of telling tales; but also to take a first part, which was once left unfinished for want of understanding, and add a second by virtue of the wisdom of years, and, thereby, to complete a Night's Entertainment.

It is my wish that you read the first part so that, having seen it, you may be as one who has not seen it; and that you see the other so that, having seen it, you may be as one who cannot forget the sight.[44]

Regine

Alaeddin The Chosen/The Wonderful Lamp[45]

Part One

In a city of the cities of the world, there dwelt one who was successful as a hosier but a failure as a man. And though he had many children, he had really but one son — Alaeddin. Now this boy had been from infancy, a distant soul, taken more to living in his own imagination than in the common world of others. He was a special character, obviously marked for some extraordinary fate which could neither be duplicated nor understood by those around him. When he reached his tenth year, his father, the hosier, inclined to teach the boy his own trade, for he lacked both the spirit and insight to expend himself upon teaching Alaeddin some work or craft other than his own, an apprenticeship closer, perhaps, to Alaeddin's special nature. Singularly unsuited as Alaeddin was for the life of a hosier, he would not, indeed could not, submit himself to his father's instruction. No sooner would the old man bring the lad into his shop than Alaeddin would await his father's leaving it for some purpose, such as to meet a creditor, and run off at once to idle in the splendid city gardens. Such was his case. Counsel and castigation were to no avail; nor would he obey the implorings of either parent that he learn a trade. Alaeddin's rebellious indolence caused such sadness and sorrowing for his father that the old man soon sickened and died. When his mother saw that her spouse had diseased, and that her son was to her useless and unmanageable, she sold the shop and all of its contents and took to the simpler, more menial profession of spinning cotton cloth. By this toilsome industry she fed herself and found food for her son, Alaeddin the Chosen, who, seeing himself freed from the severities of his father, increased in distance and spirit from home, falling in with low characters and lower habits. One day, as he was wandering about the quarter where the vagabonds and women of low repute dwell, there appeared a man, pale with age and strangely holy. He was, in fact, a Magician. Entering the quarter, he approached Alaeddin and stood gazing hard upon him, carefully considering his appearance. Now this Magician bore a striking resemblance to the long-since-departed father of Alaeddin, whose image had begun to fade from his son's memory but was reborn, by the startling magic of reincarnation, in the form of this Magician. After narrowly considering Alaeddin, he said, "Verily, this is the lad I need and to find whom I have left my natal land." Alaeddin was confused and amazed at his selection, and asked, "Why have you chosen me as the object of your coming?" "How canst thou, O my son," replied the Magician in a soft voice saddened by emotion, "question me so, after recognizing in me the image of thy father, my brother; and how must I answer when blood hideth not from blood but hath revealed to me that thou art my nephew, son of my brother, and I knew thee amongst all the lads." Then he clasped Alaeddin to his bosom crying, "O my son, I have none to condole with now save thyself; and thou standest in stead of thy sire. Take these coins to your mother and together plan to eat the evening meal in reunion with me." Whereupon Alaeddin returned home straightway, and with his mother prepared a succulent supper in welcome of this exiled relation. On the appointed evening, after much wailing and lamentation for the departed father, which certified his ancestry, the Magician related how he had journeyed into foreign lands, wandering wildly from his native stead until, moved by the yearnings of old age for beholding his brother once more, he entered the streets of the town only to behold at once his brother's son, the legacy bequeathed by Destiny that "Whoso leaveth issue is not wholly dead."

And then, with the intention of completing his deceitful tale, the Magician turned to Alaeddin saying, "O my son, what hast thou learned in the way of work and what is thy business?" Alaeddin was deeply shamed and sheepish and hung his head. But his mother spoke out, "He knows nothing at all. All day long he idles away his time in selfish and useless enterprise; and I, his mother whom he knows not, am abandoned by him but also enjoined by duty to provide him with daily bread, when I require to be provided! He does not come near to me except at meal times and none other. Indeed, I am thinking of locking the house and never again opening the door to him, but leaving him to go and seek a livelihood whereby he can live. For I have no longer strength to toil and wait for him to become a dutiful son." Hearing these words, the Magician turned to Alaeddin and said, "Tis for thee a shame that thy mother, a woman in years, should struggle to maintain and support thee. Now, surely, that thou hast grown to man's estate it becometh thee to devise some means whereby thou canst live as a man, independent and respectable." Then the Magician offered to establish and aid Alaeddin with all he could in any calling or handicraft which would suit the boy's fancy and would provide him with a man's proper calling. But when the Magician saw that Alaeddin kept silent, he knew that this child wanted no ordinary occupation and was wholly ill-disposed to aspire in the common way to achieving respectability. "O my son, son of my brother, if despite all I say, you still dislike to learn or practice a craft, I will open thee a merchant's store already furnished with the costliest stuffs, and thou shalt become at once famous amongst the folks in the marketplace where thou shalt give and take and buy and sell." At this,

Alaeddin smiled and said that he was content to be a trader
in the marketplace, one of those who dress handsomely
and fare delicately.[46] The Magician replied, "O my son,
son of my brother, prove thyself a man and, if Fate be
kind, tomorrow I will take thee to the city and from the
clothier's shop containing all kinds of suits most sump-
tuous, you shall choose what pleaseth thee; from thence
we shall travel to the Baths where you shall enjoy the
most delicate of favors; from thence we shall fare forth
into the central city and into the marketplace where you
shall become familiar with the folk and their ways, and
also with all of the religious places, the noble buildings, the
King's Palace and the merchant's area. We shall invite sun-
dry traders to come and sit with us for supper in a cook's
shop, and we shall dine off platters of silver, eating and
drinking until it is sufficient. Then we shall go our ways
until the morrow." So saying, the Magician departed.
Alaeddin was so thrilled that he did not sleep at all that
night, but wandered restlessly about the house, his imagination and all of his senses tuned to a very high pitch. When
it was dawn, the Magician appeared and with Alaeddin departed for the city where each and every promise made to
the boy was fulfilled. After they ate and drank and night
had fallen, the Magician rose up and led Alaeddin back to
his mother saying, "Tomorrow I will come again to thee
betimes and take thee for a pleasant stroll, this time to the
gardens without the city which haply you may hitherto
not have beheld." And so it was. Early the next morning,
the Magician arrived and appeared at the door even more
strikingly the image of Alaeddin's father, embracing his
son and kissing him. Then, as they were about to leave, the
Magician took Alaeddin's hand and said "O my son, this

day will I show thee a sight thou never sawest in all thy
life." And so saying, they passed through the city gate.
The Magician led Alaeddin on a promenade through the
gardens and pointed out for his pleasure all of the fine
sights, particularly the marvelous high-builded pavillions.
So they strolled, stopping to stand and stare, the Magician
speaking long and heatedly about the awesome spectacles,
and Alaeddin wondrous and intent upon each word.[47]
And they ceased not to stroll about, back and forth, and
around again until they became weary. Then they entered
one of the grandest gardens which was near at hand, a
place that delighted the heart and dazzled the sight. Here
they sat by a lakelet to relieve their fatigue and to eat from
a bag of dried fruits and victual. As soon as the bag was
emptied, the Magician said, "Arise my son, and be thou
reposed and let us stroll onwards a little and reach the end
of our walk." Thereupon Alaeddin arose and the Magician
trod with him from garden to garden until they left all of
the gardens behind them. Still onward they trod their
weary way[48] until Alaeddin, who had never left the city
gate and never had walked such a long distance from home,
said, "O uncle, where are we going? We have left all of the
familiar sights behind us, and have reached the cold, barren
hill country; and if the way is still long, I have no strength
for walking. I am ready to fall with fatigue. Before us there
is nothing, so let us go back and return to the city." Said
the Magician, "No, O my son, this is the right road; nor are
the gardens ended, for we are going to look at one which
hath ne'er its like amongst those of the Kings, nor canst
one such as this even be imagined. Gird thy courage to
walk. Thou art now a man or thou shalt surely become
one." With this admonition compelling him, Alaeddin

strode on until he reached the site intended by the Magician, who had journeyed from the city to the deserts and back again solely for the sake of this final ordeal. "Sit my son, and take thy rest, for this is the spot we are seeking and soon I will divert thee by displaying marvel beyond the range of matter." Hearing these words, Alaeddin forgot his fatigue in deep wonder about his uncle's intentions. Presently, the Magician brought out from his breast pocket a wooden box which opened from the top, and from whose inner chamber he drew all he needed of incense. Then he fumigated and conjured and adjured, muttering words in no recognizable human language. And presently, the earth broke open in repeated bursts of thick gloom, and the heavens trembled. Alaeddin was petrified; and he rose upwards like a lightning bolt and tried to fly. He had been for so long sheltered within the city gate that even his unbounded imagination and fondness for adventure could not have sustained him in the midst of such extraordinary happenings. When the Magician saw Alaeddin attempting to flee, he became furious, for without the lad, all his work, his conjurings, and adjurings, his long, arduous journeys would have been wasted. It was his fate that he could not possess the hidden hoard which he sought except by means of Alaeddin, who alone was Chosen for this treasure. This hoard, buried so far beyond the reach even of kings, so far that even the outermost deserts are cities to where it rests, was stored in the name of Alaeddin. So as Alaeddin was attempting to escape, the Magician had no recourse but to deal him a terrible blow upon the head leaving him to swoon to the ground until, by magic, he revived him. "O my son," said the Magician, "I struck thee because here lieth a hoard which will make you rich in such measure that not even Kings would be richer than yourself, an Enchanted Treasury of immense value and good, which hath been kept just for thee, and yet you intended to leave it and flee. O my son, it is my intent to make you a man; therefore do not disobey, for that I am thine uncle and like unto thy father. Obey me in all that I bid thee, and shortly, so shortly as a butterfly's life is short, thou shalt forget all this travail and toil, whenas thou shalt be joyous continuously in the marvelous realm that I shall make available to thee. Collect thyself, and behold now this marble slab wherein is fixed a copper ring. Set thy hand upon the ring and raise the slab, for you, and none other amongst the folk, hath power to lift it." Alaeddin, dazed with wonder, and rejoicing over his singular fate, approached the ring as commanded, but answered, "O uncle, this ring is too heavy for me. I cannot raise it single-handed, for I am young in years and weak. So come forward and lend me your own strength." The Magician replied, "O my son, we shall find it impossible to do aught if I assist thee, and all our efforts would be in vain. If you would set thy hand upon the ring and while pulling cease not to pronounce thy name and the names of thy father and mother, it shall rise at once to thee nor shall thou feel its weight." And lo! the stone was raised just as the Magician had bidden. Throwing the marble slab aside, there appeared before Alaeddin's eyes a deep cave, the blackest pit imaginable. Then the Magician charged Alaeddin, "Descend these seven stairs into yonder vault with all care; and when thou reachest bottom thou shalt find a space divided into seven halls; and in each of these thou shalt see jars of gold and silver, and other matter precious beyond measure. Beware, however, lest thou take aught therefrom, or touch them, or allow thy gown to brush the walls or their contents. Leave them without tarrying for a single moment along the way,[49] until thou reachest the seventh hall. Wouldst thou do anything contrary to these orders, thou shalt at once be transformed into a black stone. A door will appear within the seventh hall which leads out of it, a door of marble as burdensome as the slab at the top entrance, except if thou makest the same pronouncements as thou hast now made. Then thou shalt pass through that door into a Garden adorned everywhere with fruit-bearing trees.[50] Pass through this Garden by the only open path until thou reachest a ladder. At the top of this ladder there hangs a Lamp. Mount the ladder and take that Lamp, and place it in the pocket closest to thy heart. Once the Lamp is safely in thy breast pocket, thou are permitted to pluck from the trees, lift from the jars, and partake of the richness of the seven halls in whatever measure thou pleaseth, for the whole world and its greatest treasures are thine so long as the Lamp is in thy possession." When the Magician ended his long charge to Alaeddin, he drew from his finger a seal ring bearing the impress of a candle flame and slipped it upon Alaeddin's forefinger saying, "O my son, this signet ring shall free thee from all pain and fear which may befall or threaten a man; but remember that its powers are limited, and its scope pertains to what is human, so make only the proper use of it. Go now, down the steps into the cave, and fear not, for thou art now a man and no longer a child." Accordingly, Alaeddin descended into the cave where, in fear and trembling, with body strained to the purpose, and attention focused to a pin's point, he did precisely what the Magician had commanded. After retrieving the Lamp and returning down the ladder,

Alaeddin walked back to the Garden where he sat entranced, gazing at the trees which sang out in voices of birds, glorifying in splendid songs the Power and Majesty of their Great Creator. Alaeddin strolled in amazement through the Garden gaping at sights which bedazzled his senses and astounded his young mind. Jewels of inestimable value hung, instead of fruits, from the trees, and scattered along the ground were trinkets of precious metals as pure as light. Never before had he beheld things such as these, nor was he old enough to estimate or understand the worth of such valuables. So instead of treating them as one more knowledgeable in matters such as these might, he gathered all he could into his breast pockets to use as glass playthings and ornaments for idle hours. He plucked them in great quantities, cramming them into the pockets and folds of his clothing, until wholly laden down, he passed back again through the seven halls to the exit, whereupon he began the upward climb. But the very last step was higher than all of the others; and he was so burdened, that he could not mount it alone and unassisted. So he called out to the Magician, "Lend me your hand and aid me in the climb." But the Magician answered, "O my son, give me the Lamp and lighten thy load. It is the Lamp which weighs thee down." Alaeddin answered, "O uncle, it is not the Lamp at all, but all of the other souvenirs which fill my pockets. Though I cannot reach the Lamp at present, you shall have it as soon as I reach the upper ground." But the Magician, in his haste to have the Lamp would not be put off; instead, he persisted in demanding what Alaeddin was unable to give. He went into a rage, more and more furiously demanding the Lamp which lay out of reach in Alaeddin's pocket. Concluding that his fury was in vain, and exhausted by his efforts, the Magician lost all hope of winning the Lamp; for this youth had won victory through ignorance. In his anger and despair, seeing that all his travels and schemes and hopes were wasted, he cast a spell over the cave which then, to a crash of thunder and a flash of cold light, receded back into the ground leaving Alaeddin in the bowels of the earth to perish and die. With his highest expectations and plans foiled, the Magician retreated into faraway lands, forlorn and angry. Alaeddin, seeing the earth close up over him, began shouting and praying to his uncle to help him out. But however loudly he cried, he heard no answer. And he finally concluded that this self-styled uncle was nothing to him but a liar and a wizard, bent only upon destroying him. Then poor Alaeddin despaired of life, and finding all the doors to the halls and gardens shut and locked, he sorrowed that there was no escape for him. Trapped in the bowels of the earth, he began to weep and lament like one who has lost every hope, and he returned to sit disconsolately upon the steps by which he first entered the cave. But Destiny had ordained that Alaeddin had been presented with a gift, a seal ring with the impress of a candle upon it, a ring which, though limited in power and pertinent only to what was human, might be the means of his escape. For while he sat weeping and lamenting over his state, sinking ever more deeply into misery, he began to rub his hands together as humans are wont to do in woeful desperation, and while so doing, he chanced to rub the ring; when, lo and behold! A spirit appeared from within a dark mist saying, "I am the slave of the ring; ask whatsoever you want; and seeing that the signet of my lord be upon your finger, I am at your command." Remembering what the Magician had said when presenting him with the ring, Alaeddin recovered his spirits and rejoiced, crying, "O slave of the lord of the ring; I wish to be set back upon the face of the earth, that I might dwell again in my familiar surroundings, in my native land." The words hardly had left his lips before the earth parted and he found himself outside the cave in full view of the upper world. But having spent many days shut up in the dense blackness of the underground pit, Alaeddin's eyes were pained by the sheen of sunlight, and it was a long while before he adjusted to the glare and recovered his bearings. Gradually, turning in all directions, eyes opening and closing, he saw in the distance the vague outlines of what were the gardens outside the city gate. Focusing upon these shadows, he recognized the road which led him to the cave, and, stumbling over to it, he made his way toward town. The road grew more and more familiar as he passed upon it, until stepping across the threshold into the city, he spied his own home. Upon seeing his mother once more, he was overcome by the stress of joy at having escaped; and the memory of his dreadful experience and the tortures of it, along with the pangs of hunger and fatigue, caused him to fall upon her in a faint. Now though Alaeddin had not been a son of great devotion to his mother, she was yet, herself, a devoted mother who hastened to the aid of him who had too often abandoned her; and she tended to his needs by placing him upon her bed where for many hours he slept a long-overdue sleep. Upon awakening, Alaeddin related his strange adventure to his mother who sat listening to him wide-eyed and incredulous. She might surely have attributed such a wild tale to her son's over-active imagination except that upon completing his story, Alaeddin emptied his garments of the dazzling gems, and drew the Lamp from his breast pocket. Alaeddin's mother, believing the Lamp to have enough value only to be sold for the price of a meal, began polishing it with sand in order to enhance its value and thus bring a better price. But she had only just begun, when out from its inner chamber an apparition of immense size and impressive bearing emerged, a Spirit whose great size seemed to burst the walls of the modest dwelling. "Say whatsoever thou wantest of me," spoke the Spirit. "Here am I thy Slave; and not I alone but all the Slaves of the Wonderful Lamp serve you." The old woman was speechless and she shook with terror at the nightmarish vision. Alaeddin, seeing what had happened, took the opportunity to demonstrate the truth of his tale. He snatched the Lamp from the stiff fingers of his mother, who was paralyzed with fear, saying, "O Slave of the Lamp; it is my desire that you bring us something to eat; and make it a feast beyond compare." The Spirit disappeared, and in an instant returned with a tray of virgin silver upon which rested twelve golden platters filled with all manner of delicacies. Upon these also rested two silver cups surrounded by the purest and most delicate of wines. Then the Spirit vanished. Alaeddin's mother stood marveling at the feat and replied, "You were speaking the truth, my son; this must be the same Spirit who saved you from death when you were buried beneath the earth." "No, mother," said Alaeddin, "This is not he who saved me then. That slave was attached to the ring upon my forefinger. He is of a far different nature and has a different function than the Slave who just appeared. This omnipotent Spirit is attached to the Lamp." Upon hearing this explanation, the old woman cried, "This demon who appeared before me, frightening me almost to death, is attached to the Lamp?" "Yes," answered Alaeddin. And she replied, "O my son, by the milk wherewith I suckled you, throw this cursed Lamp away; rely not upon such occult power but upon what strengths are within you and upon the good earth. In my heart I know that this Lamp will bring us terror and suffering. But do, my son, whatever you will. For myself, I wish never to see the Lamp again nor ever to confront the frightful spectacle which issues from it." So Alaeddin, in deference to his mother's wish, hid the Lamp from view. But he did not cease asking its Slave to continue to grant to him and his parent all that was necessary to live well; in fact, to fare better and better. And the Spirit of the Lamp continued to do as Alaeddin desired. Now, because of his increasingly respectable status in life, due in full measure to the gifts of the Lamp, Alaeddin began to frequent the society of responsible men: the merchants, jewellers, and goldsmiths of the marketplace. In fact, it became his practice to spend the greater part of each day making himself familiar with the townsfolk and winning their favor.[51] For hours he would enquire in great detail about buying and selling, about the dear and the cheap as well as engaging in more familiar and friendly intercourse, until the name of "Alaeddin" was held in high esteem throughout the town, and the face of Alaeddin was immediately recognizable by its inhabitants. Then one day, as the sun was setting and Alaeddin began his walk from the marketplace to his home on its edge, he heard the words of the town crier proclaiming: "By command of our Master, the King of the Time and the Lord of the Age, let all the folk lock up their shops and stores and retire within their houses until a full day has passed, for the King's daughter

94

shall tomorrow visit this town to take lessons in song and voice from one of our own. Whosoever shall disobey this order, and conduct business as usual, shall be punished with death." When Alaeddin heard the proclamation, he could not help feeling impelled to catch sight of the Princess, especially since she had gained a reputation for unexcelled beauty. As he wound his way home, he deliberated upon a way to study her and yet to evade the terrible punishment consequent upon conducting business as usual. Finally, he contrived to take a place across from the entrance of the hall where the Princess was to take her lessons, a place suitably hidden from her, except for a small window whereby she would not be hidden from him.[52] Here it was, in a small cook's shop, that he sat in waiting, until, late in the afternoon, the Princess came into view, escorted by a Jew who, in virtue of his industry and talent, was reputed to have passed from the lowly state of a peddler to that of the wealthiest merchant in the district.[53] The Princess walked through the quarter with bowed head and eyes hidden by a dark veil.[54] But, as she approached her destination, she lifted the veil and looked all about her at her surroundings. From the moment that Alaeddin saw her face so directly revealed, he was weak. His mind fragmented, and his senses were dazed by her heavenly beauty. He was at once, and most assuredly, in love; and when his beloved passed ever-too-swiftly out of sight, he returned home in a state of turmoil and ecstasy. Alaeddin's mother, observing her son's strange behavior, took it for the delirium of some grave illness, and offered immediately to send for the doctor. But Alaeddin replied with an account of his beatific experience, saying that he was in no way ill, but deeply in love with the Princess; so much so that he re-

solved not to cease pursuing her until he won her for his
wife. "Have you gone mad?" replied his mother. "Remember your station in life. You are the orphan boy of a hosier
whose partial successes could not lessen by one hair his
deep suffering and that of his family. Do not forget that
you were bequeathed nothing of value to a King's daughter; and that your singular nature was unsuited for what
legacy was offered you. You have lost your reason, thinking you are an extraordinary fellow, blessed with virtues
and essentials which the King most assuredly shall require
before giving the hand of his daughter. My son, you are
only eccentric, having an inborn tendency to self torment.[55] And now this plan of yours to win the hand of
the Princess confirms my view. You are but a lone wolf,
often broody and living too much in the isolation of your
imagination. In spite of all your bustle, you achieve nothing, do not earn money or attain position or receive honors, but achieve nothing all along the line." You are a
penitent[56] with much to make up for. You must first become a man in this ordinary world before giving a single
thought to taking even a common girl for your wife."
Alaeddin listened intently to his mother's efforts at dissuasion, recognizing the truth in all she said and agreeing
in somewhat troubled tones that under ordinary circumstances, he would be a fool to venture into such love.
"But," said he, "my circumstances are now far from ordinary, for I possess a Lamp whose powers are boundless and
whose Slave is in my service so long as I can keep it. With
it, what was once impossible becomes, in the twinkle of an
eye, a fact. Without it, I am lost to the object of my yearning. With it, my marriage to the King's daughter is assured.
So take heart that I have not lost my wits, and as once you

marveled at the Power of the Lamp to feed us royally, so shall you gaze in awe as your son is soon royally wed." But his mother wept and said, "Oh, my son, be content with the ring on thy finger, and do as I ask. Destroy the lamp and with it the evil it will bring us!" From this time forward Alaeddin's preoccupation with winning the hand of his beloved was so complete that these were the last words exchanged with his mother until her death, which was attributed to accidental choking due to old age. Her death left Alaeddin completely alone in the world, enabling him to devote himself entirely to his singular purpose — to wed the Princess. Though Alaeddin himself would not have willed it, such a marriage would have fulfilled the greatest wishes of his now departed parents that he achieve worldly respectability. And he would thus unwittingly have repaid them for their struggles with his exceptional nature. To attain his end, each morning when the father of the Princess held court, Alaeddin appeared in the audience. With the aid of his Wonderful Lamp, he came attired in the finest clothes and adornments, arriving at the Palace in a splendid carriage drawn by horses unexcelled in all the King's stables. With him, he carried a porcelain bowl filled with some of the many gems he had gathered from the underground Paradise, gems which, in their brilliance alone, could have lighted the court chamber. It was no surprise that the King took notice of Alaeddin who, in virtue of his outward magnificence, needed not utter a single word to gain attention. As each day passed, the King grew more curious about the stranger in his court. He wondered why the lad came, since he made no effort at obtaining the audience usually intended by those frequenting the court. One afternoon, when the doors of the court chamber were

closed, and the King was returning to his private quarters
accompanied by his chief advisor, that same Jew who
was seen in the continual escort of the Princess and to
whom the King publicly promised her hand; he turned to
this Jew asking if he had any knowledge of Alaeddin or of
his intentions. The Jew replied that he knew not of Alaeddin in particular; but he did assuredly know of men such as
he, who were actors and lunatics not to be trusted or dealt
with lest they fulfill their intentions of making fools of
great men. But the King was too impressed by Alaeddin's
silent bearing and his glorious appearance to settle for this
explanation. Instead, he vowed that one morning he would
invite the young man before him and give him a hearing.
Meanwhile, however, Alaeddin was not content merely to
bedazzle the King and lure him into such an invitation. So
soon as the doors to the court were shut, he hurriedly
made his way to that street where, in late afternoon, the
Princess came for her voice lesson. Once there, he took his
place behind the window of the cook's shop to wait to
catch sight of his beloved and to learn her habits. After
many days of earnest observation, he noticed that though
she was always quick to enter the hall at the appointed
hour, her departure at dusk was delayed. In fact, she often
preferred to spend some moments alone after dismissing
her escort, the Jew, to wander briefly upon a small bridge
which spanned a deep ravine[58] just north of the city gate.
On one of these days, during the rainy season when the
ravine was near to overflowing, Alaeddin left his place behind the window of the cook's shop and followed the
Princess who was on her way alone to the bridge. In his
heart he felt that the opportunity for their meeting was at
hand. Seeing the Princess in deep, almost dreamlike con-

templation of the flow of water beneath her, Alaeddin was careful not to interfere or approach her directly, as this might only have evoked her displeasure. She was entranced by the ravine, which was completely transmuted by the annual rains. Instead of remaining upon the bridge, to hope there for a chance meeting, Alaeddin took a steep and narrow footpath down to the edge of the stream, where he stood upon some flat rocks, looking, in the matchless, sparkling clothes supplied by the Spirit of the Lamp, quite regal . . . indeed, quite like a handsome merman up from the deep.[59] Glancing up, he was able to catch a full view of the Princess whose eyes seemed to be searching for something, gazing after something at the bottom of the ravine. There was a humility in her glance which set strangely upon her royal bearing, making her look like a lowly flower belied by its bloom. Alaeddin was intoxicated; and he repeated to himself the same words which silently he spoke when first he beheld her: "She will be mine." And, by some mysterious means, these words reached her ears; for as he pronounced them to himself, he noted the trance of the Princess was broken, and she turned, as if startled, toward Alaeddin, where he stood. Then he ascended to the steep abutment just above the ravine. He called to her, and by his smooth speech and outstretched arms, enticed her to him from her position upon the bridge. Then he caught her up in his arms; and she, with her whole soul, abandoned herself to him, to his words, to his arms; not timidly, not doubtingly, not as a concession or surrender, not intoxicated by romance, but with absolute faith in him. Alaeddin stood for some moments upon the brink, leaning over the ravine with his beloved twined about him, her whole body bespeaking absolute intimacy and innocence. Many things rushed through his mind. Then he turned his eyes from her to the ravine; and as if thrust forward by some inner command, he carried her down into it, fording the stream by means of some irregularly placed rocks. Though the experience was, for the Princess, quite out of the ordinary, she made no attempt to flee, nor did she show any sign of fear. The waters were rough and swift around the rocks, and Alaeddin's balance precarious; but throughout, she maintained absolute confidence in the merman who arose from the deep to snatch her down with him into the stream.[60]

Part Two

Alaeddin must have been day dreaming, or asleep, or intoxicated, for it seemed that an eternity of time had passed before he noticed how dark the skies had become. Night had fallen, and the Princess had still to journey home, But by this time, the carriages and attendants had lost sight of their charge and had returned to the Palace to report her missing to the King. Seeing that she was abandoned, due, in large measure to his seduction, Alaeddin offered her his protection and the use of his own regal stallion for the journey home. Now at his mercy, the Princess could do nothing but agree. Safely home, they entered the Palace through the outer court chamber, where they were greeted by much commotion; for the King had come in deep worry. and agitation to publicly proclaim the disappearance of the Princess, and to summon the help of the townsfolk in the search for her. The King's jubilation at the arrival of the pair was mingled with surprise at the sight of his beloved daughter returned to him in the care of the mysterious stranger who daily appeared in his court. After showering the Princess with fatherly affection, the King embraced Alaeddin and invited him into his private quarters, where they were to celebrate the homecoming with a feast. The Jew, who because of his carelessness, had fallen out of favor with the King, became worried at the affection displayed toward Alaeddin, as well as embarrassed at having failed in his duties to his betrothed, to guard the Princess from danger. In an effort to regain his privileged place in the Royal family, the Jew began to consider how Alaeddin might be defeated. All the while the feast was celebrated, well into the following day, the Jew calculated. And when, from the private quarters, word came that Alaeddin was to be the new bridegroom, the Jew hurried to the King with a proposal. Since the greatest power possessed by the Jew was his wealth and his practical wisdom, he proposed to the King that a contest be held to determine who could best love and protect the Princess; that the victor be determined by the quality of the Palace that he could build for her, a Palace designed solely about and for her, a palace which would be the perfect setting for her beauty and grace, a Palace in which she would rule as absolute sovereign and queen, a Palace which would rival the shrines of divine worship. Since the King was fair-minded, and remembered his former promises, he agreed that these two suitors were rivals for the hand of the Princess and should be set the task of completing, as well and as rapidly as possible, the perfect Palace for the Princess. He decreed that a period of three months be set as the time of trial.

At the end of this time, or whenever one of the rivals claimed to be finished, the King would make a final judgment, and the victor would become the husband of the Princess. Soon, after the terms of the contest were set forth the Jew returned to his shop in the merchant's quarters, there to make preparations for the great task. For many long days and nights he deliberated upon the virtues and tastes of the Princess and worked drawing up plans for her Pavillion. When these were near to completion, he summoned the best tailors and spinners of cloth, the best jewellers, carpenters, stone cutters, and goldsmiths, and set them slowly, carefully to work. But Alaeddin was otherwise occupied. Once the Jew had departed, he turned to the King saying, "The building shall quickly be completed by the most diligent work of one at your service and at the feet of Her Highness, the Princess." So saying, he bade farewell to the King, and returning home, he drew the Wonderful Lamp from a rosewood box, and rubbed it once again. "Ask, O my Lord, whatsoever you want," spoke the Spirit of the Lamp. And Alaeddin replied, "I require a service of utmost significance. You must, in all urgency, build me a Palace; and it must be a marvel provided with every necessity to house the queen of the world." The Spirit replied, "To hear is to obey," And then he vanished until dawn of the following day, when Alaeddin found himself within the walls of the Palace which the Spirit of the Lamp had built in one night. All of its stones were jasper and alabaster, marble and mosaic. Its treasury was filled with all manner of gold and silver and precious gems, uncountable in quantity and inestimable in value. Alaeddin inspected the dining quarters which were fitted out in plates, dishes, spoons, and ladles, basins and covers, cups and goblets, all in precious metals. Its warehouses were piled up with chests packed with royal cloths, such as gold brocades from India and China, kim cobs and orfrayed cloth as well. Countless apartments lined its halls complete with appointments which defy description; and there were stables and harness rooms hung with costly saddles and accessories, everywhere studded with pearls and precious stones to set upon steeds whose like was not to be found in all the world. Alaeddin's Palace (if one could speak of it thus) was fully provided with slaves and with handmaids whose beauty could seduce a saint; and all this was the work of one night!! Yet the prime marvel of the Palace was an upper apartment, cut off from the rest — the strictly private quarters of husband and wife, which contained twenty-four windows all made of emeralds and rubies and other gems. However, one window of the apartment remained unfinished at the behest of Alaeddin, in deference to the power of the King, that he might assume that Alaeddin was incapable of completing it. When Alaeddin had finished the tour of the Palace and judged it fitting, he sent word by messenger to the King that his work was complete and that he was prepared for the judging. Upon receiving Alaeddin's message, the King was astonished, but he sent straightway for his advisor the Jew, to inform him that the time was at hand for judgment. The Jew was bewildered, and shook his head incredulously saying, "The man is a magician, or we have all gone mad! This cannot be! I, who have brought all of the finest workmen and materials second only to those of the King himself, have barely begun to lay the first stones! By what dreadful manner of means can Alaeddin's work be already done?" He then rose from his chair, and without yet conceding victory, he went with the King's messengers to Alaeddin's Palace (if one can speak of it thus) to assess the situation first hand. "This is a hoax, a trick, a deceit," he kept muttering to himself, until reaching the appointed place, he stopped in his tracks, awe-struck. Not far from where he stood was the King, also rapt in wonder at the sight. Alaeddin approached the dazed pair and led them inside. They considered its construction, its masonry, all jasper and carnelian, and they were struck speechless by its grandeur and opulence. Turning to the Jew, the King finally asked, "What do you say. Tell me, have you ever in your life seen anything like this amongst the mightiest of the earth's monarchs?" And the Jew replied, "O my Lord, the King, this is a feat which cannot be accomplished by the might of any man, even the greatest of monarchs, nor could the collected peoples of the whole world build such a Palace as this; indeed, no builders could be found with the talent and resource to make anything resembling it; except, as I have already offered, by the use of some dreadful magic." But the King took these words as further evidence of the Jew's envy and jealousy of Alaeddin, and he responded, "I understand what you are saying, and I know well what impels you to such unjustified words." Then the Jew, in a state of confusion and despondency, departed. But convinced of his suspicions and of his rightful place beside the Princess, as well as his deep devotion to her, he did not despair; but continued to seek ways in which he could win her back. The Jew gone, Alaeddin proceded to conduct the King to the upper apartment which was to be the most intimate and the most glorious of all the Palace apartments. There he showed its skylights, its windows, its latticed casements studded with emeralds and rubies and other costly gems. The King wandered about it gazing here and there, and finding, wherever his glance rested a wondrous sight. Then, by chance, his eyes caught sight of the window which, by design, Alaeddin had left unfinished. And noting its incompleteness, so startling beside the others, the King turned sharply to Alaeddin and asked, "My son, what is the reason why this window of this apartment was not made perfect like the others?" "O King," he replied, "the suddenness of my good fortune and the turmoil of my joy made it difficult for me to find artists for finishing it." "I have a mind to complete it myself," said the King. "Glory to the King. So shall your memory endure in your daughter's Palace," answered Alaeddin. Thereupon the King summoned his jewellers and goldsmiths and set them this task; he ordered that they be supplied from the Greater Treasury whatever they required in gold and silver and gems and precious metals to complete and perfect the unfinished window. So commanded, they then set to work. Meanwhile, in the great halls of the lower levels of the Palace, all was mirth and merriment. In celebration of the impending marriage, there was a great feast of music, dancing, eating, and drinking. The cup went round until the entire population had their fill, and then all retired to a different salon where the dessert was set forth of such fruits and sweetmeats as could satisfy the finest palette. During the taking of dessert, the King was suddenly reminded of his orders to have the window of the upper apartment completed; and feeling his pride as a King and as a father to be at stake, he implored Alaeddin and the Princess to interrupt their feasting so as to inspect the window and the progress being made upon it. So they climbed the great staircase to the very top and entered the private quarters. There they found the jewellers and gold-smiths finishing their work and preparing to depart. But the King became enraged and sorely disappointed seeing that the now-finished window was no match at all for the others, that it was no testimony to his greatness and the greatness of his love for his daughter. Promptly he ordered his slaves to seize all of the precious stones and metals from all of the noblemen of the kingdom, and he was about to command his craftsmen to resume their labors, continuing until the window reached the desired perfection. But the Princess interrupted saying, "Dear father, I am content to live in this great edifice with the window completed as it now is. Though it is not an exact match for its brothers, it yet possesses a distinctiveness and singularity which reflects your power and your devotion alone. Any further effort to refashion the window is, to me, unnecessary — positively damaging. I pray you, father, allow this window to remain finished as it has been, using the resources you alone possess." Her tone was so imploring, and when she had made her plea, she was so near to tears, that the King was persuaded to honor her request. "So it shall be," replied the King; and he ordered the workmen away. Then, turning to his daughter and future son, he said, "Let us return to our public and to the feast in your honor. Tonight we belong in the lower halls, not yet in this uppermost one." But both Alaeddin and the Princess hesitated to obey. The Princess begged to be left briefly in the private chamber so as to collect herself for she was in a far different state now from that required for merrymaking and feasting and needed some time to regain her high spirits. Alaeddin, in his turn, hesitated in silence. For the first time, he was struck by the significance of that window. He was, to the depth of his soul, repelled by the sight of the now finished, but imperfect window. He shuddered to think that it was to remain so strikingly inconsistent with the others, indeed with the Palace itself. That window was the chip on the rim of a fine porcelain bowl, a blemish upon the face of a madonna, a stain upon the collar of a King. Alaeddin stood paralyzed for a moment by his intense revulsion, and even as he began slowly to depart, he knew he could not rest until that window was destroyed and replaced by one which was perfect. Leaving the Princess to herself, the King returned to the celebration followed by a deeply disturbed Alaeddin. Now while feasting and celebrating were the order of the day in one city, a preoccupied magician in another was making a momentous discovery. News of Alaeddin's wealth and power spread quickly, and word of it had finally reached the town where the Magician lived. Upon learning of Alaeddin's fortunes, the Magician became furious, his anger and passion for revenge multiplying as the days passed. With the aid of sorcery, he learned the precise location of the Lamp, which was, where Alaeddin most recently had left it — upon the jewelled casement of the unfinished window. In great fury, and firm resolve to possess the Lamp once and for all, the Magician pronounced the words which at once transported him to the town wherein it lay. And it was his great good fortune that when he arrived, the entire population was crammed into the new Palace; and that the universal welcome which was extended by the King, along with the general revelry, assured him of safe passage into and through it. Stealthily and unnoticed he wound his way up the marble staircases toward the magnificent private apartment at the top. Upon reaching this exotic chamber, he was overjoyed to find that the door was ajar. He slipped in; and peering warily from behind a silk screen, he spied the Princess who had been left to rest in this silent, private place. Observing her innocence and frailty, he concluded that far from being an obstacle to his plan, she was perfectly suited to aid him in carrying it through. Promptly, he entered the chamber and announced, "My Lady, a thousand pardons for so rude an interruption; but my Lord Alaeddin has instructed me immediately to fetch for him a Lamp which sets upon a window casement, giving me no explanation for the reason for haste, but imploring me onward with all speed to accomplish the deed. Should you grant me but a moment, I shall have his Lamp and be off, leaving you to your privacy." The Princess, of course, knew nothing of the powers of the sacred Lamp, nor even, indeed, of its existence. Surrounded as she was by such worldly opulence and swept away by the intoxication of love, the Lamp appeared as an object of wholly ordinary quality. In fact, gazing up at it in its place upon the jewelled casement of the window, it looked positively ugly and out of place. So, being naturally timid and upset by the Magician's sudden appearance, and judging the Lamp to be of no consequence, as well as wanting only to please and to obey the wishes of her lover, she replied, "Enter; and you shall have your master's wish." She then lifted the Lamp from its place upon the casement, and deposited it with the Magician who, in the long-anticipated joy of possession, made a speedy departure, flying like a bird down the marble steps and out of the Palace. Once safely outside of the city gate, the new Lord of the Lamp summoned the Spirit to his service. "Say whatsoever thou wantest of me," spoke the Spirit; "Here am I, thy Slave." Then the Magician ordered the Spirit to transport him along with Alaeddin's Palace (if it can be so called) emptied of all its inhabitants except the Princess, to his own native land of Africa where the unique edifice would become his home and the lovely Princess his concubine. The Spirit disappeared, and in an instant, the deed was done. Before this time, the townsfolk had all returned to their homes weary with celebration, leaving the King, the Queen, Alaeddin, and the King's closest attendants to find themselves suddenly transported into the city streets with no sign whatever of the Palace or the Princess. The King was beside himself with amazement and grief. He immediately ordered Alaeddin bound and blindfolded and ready for the executioner's blade. Then, addressing Alaeddin, he said, "Where is your Palace, and where is my daughter, the core of my heart, my innocent child, the flower of my old age?" Alaeddin answered, "O, King; I do not know what has happened, but it has not been my will, and it is not my responsibility. I am not guilty of this deed, and I beg to be pardoned."[62] "You shall not be permitted to evade responsibility," answered the King. "I hold you alone accountable for this calamity. You alone know what has transpired here. And I shall pardon you only so that you may set out to find my daughter. Do not show yourself in my presence unless she is with you; and if ever I should see you alone and without her, I shall have you beheaded. For her return you shall have forty days. On the forty-first, if I am still without my daughter, I shall search the ends of the earth to find you and to kill you." So saying, he released Alaeddin, who for two days lingered about the town in the saddest state, not knowing where to go or what to do to find the Palace and the Princess. On the third day, he wandered out of the city, coming to stray through the wastelands and fields which lay beyond the city gate. It was a hungry, desperate, and weary Alaeddin who trod his lonely way in obsessive search for an unknown path. He walked aimlessly for many days and many nights until he came upon a river bank where, in deepest sorrow, he abandoned himself to despair and even thought of casting himself into the deep waters. Being however, a man more of thought than of action, and conceiving himself to be duty-bound to his mission, as well as feeling inwardly compelled to recover his estate and to perfect it, he fell instead into a fit of weeping, purging himself by the river's edge and then cleansing his face in its waters. But it happened that as he was weeping, baling up the water in his right hand, and lifting it with his fingers on the left, he chanced to rub the signet ring. In a flash, the spirit of the ring, which had once before saved his life, appeared and asked what Alaeddin desired. Alaeddin, who in his preoccupation with the powers of the Lamp, had completely forgotten this more limited spirit, was jubilant. "O Slave, I desire that you bring before me my Palace and my Princess together with everything therein." But the spirit replied, "My lord, you are demanding a service which I cannot render. This feat can only be accomplished by the Spirit of the Lamp, nor would I even dare attempt it." Alaeddin became somewhat impatient, and answered, "Well, if this matter is beyond your competence, bring me then the Lamp whose Spirit is more powerful." Hearing this, the spirit of the ring was silent; and were it not that the behavior of spirits defies description in human terms, one might have said that he was angry. Yet he replied to Alaeddin, "This too, is beyond my power, but pertains only to him who best loves the Lamp's gifts, and because of this,

would himself not rest until he possessed It." Alaeddin
was astonished to hear the spirit speaking in such a fashion,
and he rejoined, "If this matter is also beyond your competence, I shall not ask it of you; but, if you can, do this
much — transport the truest and best lover of the gifts of
the Lamp to the Palace and set him down in whatever land
it may be." The spirit of the ring, who, for one brief and
anxious moment had appeared as singularly human, now
returned to his proper mien, and hearing Alaeddin's words,
he lifted him high into the air, and in the space of a second, set him down beside his Palace (if it may be so called)
in the land of Africa. But the spirit, who knew naught but
how to obey his master's orders as they were spoken, and
having no right of his own to discriminate amongst particu-
lars, had also to provide transport to the wealthy Jew who,
because he also professed to be the truest and best lover of
the Princess (she being, in a manner of speaking, one of the
Lamp's gifts) merited the trip. In a garden beneath the
windows of the Princess' bower, Alaeddin sat in waiting,
while unknown to him, his rival, the Jew, made his way into the Palace using as a means of entry his profession as a
traveling merchant. Now the Princess, because of her sorrow at being separated from her lover and her native land,
and because of her fear of the Magician and her ignorance
about what had happened, would rise in the dense fog before dawn despite a sleepless night and would sit in tears
by her window. She was a pitiful figure, sitting there by
that finished but unfinished window surrounded by countless treasures which should have filled any maiden's heart
with gladness. She had given up eating and drinking, and
her fasting left her body pale and wasted. But her attendants did not cease in their efforts at coaxing her to eat and

in consoling her. At dawn, her favorite slave girl would enter with food and drink; and then would throw open the windows to reveal the peaceful countryside beyond them. That morning, as the slave peered out of the lattice, she caught sight of Alaeddin seated in the garden below and cried out, "O my Lady! O my Lady! Alaeddin is here seated at the foot of the wall." The Princess hurried to the window to gaze once again upon the face of her distant lover to whom she called, "Up! And come into me by the private door, for the cursed Magician has gone out to conduct his business." Then she gave orders to the slave girl to let Alaeddin in. Once inside, the pair exchanged kisses and tears. Then Alaeddin made for the unfinished window, and finding the Lamp missing from its place, said, "Before we go further, I must ask you an urgent question. A copper Lamp was placed by me upon the casement of this window. What has become of it?" Hearing this, the Princess began to sigh and weep. "O my love, it was that very Lamp which brought this calamity upon us." And she recounted all that had transpired, adding that she was informed by the Magician that he had accomplished the foul deed by the might and magic of the Lamp. "And what is your place here; and why has he brought you with him?" She replied, "Once a day he comes to visit me and tries to persuade me that you are deceased or have deserted me; that you are a deceiver, a mere pauper who was enriched by him and by means of the Lamp. He implores that I marry him, and coaxes me with promises and sweet talk. But weak as I am from despair and sorrow, I have not renounced my hope and my faith in you, nor have I, even in the smallest measure, acceded to his demands or been tempted by his seductions." "Where is the Lamp?" replied

Alaeddin. "He carries it with him always, never leaving it anywhere except upon his person; but once, when drunk with courting, he removed it from his breastpocket and displayed it before me." When Alaeddin heard this, he sighed a deep sigh of relief, and said, "Listen carefully. I shall leave you now; and I shall return only after I have changed costume; so do not wonder when you see me transformed; but order one of your slaves to stand guard by the private door, and when she sees me approach have her open it at once. I have a plan whereby to kill the Magician and retrieve my Lamp." Then Alaeddin left immediately for the marketplace, forcibly exchanging on the way, his regal clothes with those of a peasant; and there he purchased two ounces of a rare and highly potent Perfume known for its intoxicating effects, and a vial filled with two ounces of deadly poison. Then in disguise he returned to the Palace where the slave girl led him back to the private quarters. The Princess, in ignorance of Alaeddin's plan, and confused by all the terrible events, became progressively agitated, and wanted only a return to normalcy, to share once again long intimate moments with her lover. But Alaeddin had other sentiments. "Listen to me!" he said. "Empty this perfume upon your body and dress yourself in your finest velvets and lace, casting off all signs of care and turmoil. And when next the Magician comes to visit you, welcome him profusely and meet him with outstretched arms and a charming smile, and invite him to dine with you. Moreover, tell him that you have finally forgotten Alaeddin and your homeland, and that you have come to love him more than you had loved Alaeddin, displaying all the while your great charm and beauty. Then ask him to toast you with wine again and again until he becomes careless; then drop the contents of this vial of poison into his next cup and no sooner shall he drink it, than he will fall back dead, and I shall be able to retrieve the Lamp which is rightfully mine, and so to perfect our estate." Hearing these words, the Princess was bewildered and could not imagine herself performing such a vicious deed as this, even though it was perpetrated upon an evil Magician. She could not comprehend why Alaeddin desired the possession of the Lamp before the restoration of their love, nor why she must suffer humiliation as the means by which he was to recover it. Might not the Magician overtake her, convinced as he had to be of her affection and surrender? What if he, as shrewd as he was, discovered the scheme and vindictively took her life instead? It seemed to the Princess that Alaeddin was more than outwardly transformed; that some mysterious change had taken place during their separation. She could not understand how his awful plan and her involvement in it could be an expression of his love; nor could she conceive how her willingness to obey could be an expression of her own love. But matters were so pressing, and her state was so intolerable, that she could do nothing but follow his instructions, hoping beyond hope to be saved. Alaeddin departed, waiting by the private door for the moment when he was to recover the Lamp. The Princess summoned her servant who proceded to dress her in her finest clothes, to adorn her with fabulous jewels and trims, and to perfume her from the exotic bottle which Alaeddin had purchased, incognito, that morning. When done, the Princess sat upon her chair looking quite as if she were waiting to welcome her truest lover. But, in fact, she sat upon the brink of terror. As ordered, she sent a servant girl with a message

to the Magician that she was prepared to see him. Now
during the time when Alaeddin was engaged in these elaborate preparations, the Jew was occupied in carrying out
his own plans. By rather direct means, he entered the
Palace as a traveling merchant to display his wares to the
Magician. The Jew, in the course of offering a very long
and narrow piece of cotton cloth, worked it round and
round the body of the Magician, all the while engaged in
heated conversation, and indicating with profuse compli-
ments its suitability for him, until, reaching his collar, he
pulled the cloth up in one sharp jerk, and strangled the
evil man. Just before he fell dead, the Magician had time
to clutch furiously for the Lamp in his breast pocket. But
he died as his hands clasped it in a grip of desperation. The
Jew, wondering at this curious effort, removed the Lamp
from the Magician's pocket as if it were a souvenir from a
kill, to present ot the Princess, and proceeded with it to
the room where she sat in dreadful anticipation of the
Magician's visit. When her old lover opened the door and
entered the room, she was confounded by the sight of a
wholly unexpected face; but she fast became joyous in
greeting him who relieved her from the dread of becoming
a murderess, and protected her from the foul clutches of
the Magician. For many intimate moments this lover sat
with his arms about the Princess, consoling her with his
protection, assuring her of his undying and untiring affection, and of his dedication to the task of removing her
from this foreign land and returning her home. Wrapped in
the strong, warm embrace of her old lover, the Princess
felt as if she were reborn, as if she had awakened from a
terrible nightmare, as if she were home despite the fact
that she was still many miles away. She raised her eyes to

this man, her old, and now her new lover and kissed him gently, the sweet tears of joy falling singly from her eyes; and then she said, "You have come," and he replied, "I have come." The two lovers then began their preparations to depart, gathering the few belongings of the Princess along with whatever was necessary for the trip home. As they were about to leave the upper apartment, her lover remembered the Lamp that he retrieved from the dead Magician, and removed it from his pocket to give to the Princess. But as soon as she set eyes upon it, a flood of past memories swept through her mind, and she immediately averted her face. So her lover, knowing as well as a lover can the meaning of this gesture, thought better of his plan, and instead, quickly placed the Lamp out of sight, outside the private door which led to the outer gardens, and behind which Alaeddin stood in waiting. Then the pair left the Palace by means of the public stairways and exits which trailed down its center. When Alaeddin saw the door open, and the Lamp placed beside him, he pounced upon the precious object as a hunter attacks his prey. For some time, he stood hypnotized by the act of possession, caressing the Lamp, examining its every side, and curve and mark, even speaking to it in the soft tones of love. Then, placing it with great care in his breast pocket, he went, at last, inside through the private door to reunion with the Princess. But she had already departed. Alaeddin searched the entire Palace, looking everywhere, calling her name, persuading, cajoling, commanding her out of her hiding place. But no response was forthcoming except the familiar sound of Alaeddin's own voice echoing, echoing, echoing, from stone to jewel to precious metal, his own words. Finally, in great weariness, Alaeddin sat down with his

Lamp upon the bed in the private chamber, and called
forth the Spirit. "Here am I thy Slave; and not I alone, but
all the Slaves of the Wonderful Lamp. Ask, O my Lord
whatsoever you want," spoke the Spirit. And Alaeddin replied, "It is my desire that my beloved, the Princess, be
restored to me from wherever or whatever condition she
is presently to be found." But the Spirit answered, "O my
Lord, you are demanding a service which even I cannot
render. This feat cannot be accomplished by any Spirit
alone; nor even by all of the Spirits collectively, nor would
I, nor all of the Slaves of the Wonderful Lamp together,
even dare to attempt it." Alaeddin, amazed at this declaration, and incapable of understanding why his order could
not be carried through, fell into deep confusion, not knowing what to say or to do next. He sat upon the bed staring
blankly into space, and then, looking about him here and
there, the magnificence of the Palace began again to impress itself upon him. His troubled heart was consoled by
its beauty and grandeur. Then his eyes chanced once again
upon the finished but unfinished window; and, as in the
past, it appeared to him utterly repugnant, needing to be
at once obliterated and perfected. Turning to the Spirit,
Alaeddin changed his orders: "It is my desire that this
window which was once left unfinished now be finished."
"To hear is to obey," replied the Spirit; and in an instant,
a feat of which all the best artists in the world were incapable, was accomplished. "Things are now as they
should be," said Alaeddin to himself, as he gazed upon
each of the twenty-four windows one-by-one, until his turmoil and fatigue were lulled by the comfort of pleasure;
and he lay down upon the bed in the most perfect Palace
ever created, and went to sleep.

During this long sleep, which lasted beyond the opening of eyes, the Princess and her lover were married; and when the King died they lived for many years as rulers of their native land in peace and happiness, loved by all of their subjects. Alaeddin's fortunes multiplied many times over; his fame and power spread to every corner of the world. He was generous to all he met, and went about traveling for a few short years in high style. But as the years passed, he took to remaining more and more in his Palace until he became something of a recluse, refusing to leave the upper apartment. Many women tried him with their virtues, but he never married. The Princess was often favored with communications from him. At first, she responded sympathetically, even wishfully. But it is said that after ten years, not even the best of memories can altogether accurately retain the image of one departed.[62]

Once there was a Lamp called the Wonderful; when it was rubbed, a Spirit appeared. Joy! But love is the only true wonderful Lamp; rub it with passion, and behold! Many spirits appear; and one spirit is a servant; so wish upon that spiritual Lamp, all ye whose spirit serves a wish![63]

1843 — 1848

From my reader (if I dare speak of such) I would request the favor of a forgetful remembrance accorded me in passing, a token that it is me he remembers.

CONCLUDING UNSCIENTIFIC POSTSCRIPT,
Acknowledgment.

Editor's Note to the Letters of "That Single Individual"

This, the fourth set of papers, I am able to present almost entirely as I found them, except for one interesting modification. While the previous three groups of manuscripts seemed to require additional material and development, this fourth set seemed to call for subtraction.

Attached to and included amongst many of the letters were various other documents. There were, for example, many clippings from Copenhagen newspapers: *The Corsair, The Fatherland, North and South,* which were either written by or about Kierkegaard. There were various caricatures of Kierkegaard sketched in pencil, and signed "That Individual," which were far more brutal than any which appeared in *The Corsair.* In addition, there were many long but incomplete outlines of projected analyses of some of the central concepts in Kierkegaard's works; many short and incomplete attempts at love songs and poems; and many largely blank sheets of paper bearing clues that a letter was to appear upon them. Reading the complete set of papers which SK had apparently received and/or collected from "That Single Individual," one who once was called Kierkegaard's reader, it seemed to me that the writer's intentions were better served and communicated by omitting everything but the letters.

So I present all of the letters of one of Kierkegaard's readers intact. Read without the notes, pictures, clippings, and abstract analyses which accompanied them, they seem to trace the response of a reader who begins by accepting, indeed loving, an author, and ends by rejecting him absolutely. The first letter was evidently written after the publication of *Either/Or* in 1843, when Kierkegaard's concealment, in the form of pseudonymity, had begun. The last letter was probably written after the publication of *The Concluding Unscientific Postscript* in 1846. In this book, Kierkegaard confessed his identity with and responsibility for the pseudonyms. During the years between 1843 and 1846, Regine was engaged and married, and *Either/Or, Repetition, Fear and Trembling, Philosophical Fragments, The Concept of Dread, Stages on Life's Way,* and *The Concluding Unscientific Postscript* were published. During this period, Kierkegaard was attacked in the newspaper *The Corsair* and responded with attack in the newspaper *The Fatherland.* In 1847 SK wrote in his journal, "God be praised that I was subject to the attack of the rabble. I have now had time to arrive at the conviction that it was a melancholy thought to want to live in a vicarage, doing penance in an out-of-the-way place, forgotten. I now have made up my mind quite otherwise." In 1848 Kierkegaard noted that his health was poor and he was convinced that he would soon die; in the same year, he wrote that *The Point Of View For My Work As An Author* was "as good as finished." The events of significance which occurred in these three years, having their own peculiar bearing (or lack of it) upon the letters from the reader, I include for your information — to make of them in interpreting "That Individual's" relationship with SK what you will.

Victor Eremita[64]
c/o Reitzel's
Copenhagen

Dear Victor:

Will you pardon my presumption in addressing you so intimately? It serves, I assure you, only to compensate for the distance which separates us. Would that there were a better way for me to make contact with you than through the public intermediary, Giodwad.[65] But where are you . . . to be reached directly?

It is not my practice to write to authors; indeed, it is no longer my practice to read books; I suppose for the very reason that you must have written yours — that they invariably fail to be anything more than mere pulp. My education occurs in the streets and cafes and in the bedrooms of Copenhagen. Each moment, each act of existence, builds my library. I, too, am one "without book," and I address you as a kindred spirit, with the appropriate informality. I address you, Victor, as a man who I do not know, as well as a man who I know well.

I do not know what impelled me to purchase your book some weeks ago; no less to proceed to read it! I happened to be taking a customary stroll through the center of town, after spending an equally customary afternoon in various cafes, engaged there in frenzied disputes over literary and aesthetic matters — a typical, thoroughly sensuous day filled with romance and poetic interests. I seem inexorably drawn to intense personal involvement in any and every occasion which promises or invites the Beautiful, either intellectually or physically.[66] Yet this was not always so. I gained the freedom I needed to pursue the good life sometime back, by the rather delicate seduction of a wealthy heiress (a novelty, since I have a definite predilection for kitchen maids) from which I profited so significantly (by means of which I shall refrain from speaking) that I was immediately able to retire from the world of respectable men at the remarkable age of twenty-three.[67] Moreover, successes of this envious sort have advantageous consequences. I achieved, along with my freedom, an almost sacred position in the eyes of women, a high status in social and intellectual circles, and an inward sense of personal vitality and expertise. Many women try me with their wiles; I am in great demand at cafe tables and intimate parties; I am popular with my peers and the envy of the masses. So, as I swaggered along that fateful afternoon, expertly tailored, a devil of a fellow, with the sound of change keeping a loose beat in my pockets, I felt that my life could not have been better; there was nothing missing in it. I was satisfied!

But strangely enough, all the while that I was swelling with self-satisfaction, sensing to the tips of my fingers my virility, my power, I was traversing the very same path, making the very same journey that, some months before, I was daily, almost hourly driven to make out of despair. For just a short time ago, my energy was all but completely dissipated, my finances depleted, my reputation as an aesthete on the verge of collapse, my lovers proving to be mere transients, my friends mere associates. Everything I touched seemed to turn to black stone[68] and I fell continually to musing about death. So soon as this intellectual

124

dance with death began, I would up and be off on another promenade through the streets of Copenhagen, pacing, trodding, wending my way toward the dance's end. What a different quality my walking had then! Each step was an effort at real motion which might change my place from an old to a new world; but my steps managed only to lead from one oblivion to the next. Why, now that my life had undergone a metamorphosis, had achieved a degree of perfection unrivaled by my fellows, why was I still retracing the very same route of despair I had repeatedly made during those earlier, miserable days? I might have explained the repetition[69] on the basis of habit alone, except for the events of that late afternoon and their consequences — events which convinced me that a far different explanation lay behind it.

Well, anyway, I was not entertaining any of these thoughts on my way that afternoon; I was not thinking at all. I was bathing in the warm sun of contentment, in the heat of the moment, which had for so long been absent from my cold climate. I passed down many streets, by many shops, around many of those people who, for their own reasons and lack of them, were mulling about town. My eyes rested nowhere in particular, and my attention was so diffuse that it melted under the heat into a vague sensation of vitality. I must have been rising like steam, somewhere above the cobblestones.

Then I saw the book in the tiny window of Reitzel's.[70] Rather, I should say, it saw me; for it was as if my attention were taken by the collar and held, dangling and befuddled, in air. On the book's cover were the words, "Either/Or." The sharp glare of those words cut through the center of my awareness. Those words, "Either/Or," were an offense, an insult hurled at me from some invisible lips. I remember feeling quite perturbed, and then resentful about the perturbation; for it seemed to me to be a wholly useless and trivial discomfort. The sight of those words created a sharp split in my condition, a needless crack in my self-possession. Two ordinary, even insipid words etched in gold: "Either/Or." They introduced doubt into the assumption that my life was complete; they threatened me with the suggestion that there was something that might still be entertained, some left-over morsel of an alternative. An alternative to what I had taken to be perfection? My successful life; was I being tricked? Was something being withheld from me; What was it? What was this "Or?" What was the "Either?"

Driven equally by revenge against the words, as by a personal interest in their significance, I stormed into Reitzel's and bought the book. I was becoming angrier and angrier about my sense of being trapped by the thing . . . by any book; and for so obscure, so elusive a reason. I continued my walk, bearing the book upon my person as one bears an umbrella to an outdoor dance on a clear day. I could not have arrived at a cafe soon enough to set it down. But as I am a practical, as well as a curious, person who does not waste his money upon useless ornaments, especially when they are of a largely intellectual nature, I sat down alone at a table and began to examine my purchase.

Now speaking candidly, I am an ordinary man so far as creative talent and intelligence are concerned. I, myself, am no more than an appreciator and commentator upon the Beautiful. However, I do think that I am uncommonly open and receptive to ideas and creations of all sorts, and in this, many cuts above my fellows. But, considering even my catholic interests and tolerance for the extraordinary (which has resulted, as one might expect, in having been the recipient of more than my share of oddities, and the confidant of far too many eccentrics), your book, *Either/Or*, was the queerest, the oddest thing I have laid eyes upon to date. It was truly incomparable, bearing not the slightest relation to anything familiar. And yet — and this is what so astonishes me — every single line of it struck me as absolutely pertinent to my own life; struck me not in any clear or discursive way, not in any way I could explain, but in an absolutely direct hit, on a wholly intuitive level. At one and the same time, I failed utterly to understand the significance of your book, and I also felt touched to the core of my being by its content. This contradiction has evoked in me a mood which will not disappear — the strangest sort of boredom! Persistent boredom!

I shall not be more specific than to say that the pains to which you went in fictionalizing your "Seducer" were misplaced. Such a man lives! But you know this too, do you not? You must understand what you have written, and in what manner you sought to touch the lives of other men, to touch my life, in particular. Specificity of analysis is scholarship; I am uninterested, and it is not your point at all, is it? Analysis would not come near to expressing the important sense in which I feel so close to you that I have taken to writing you this letter.

In spite of the tendency to explain, and the information I have just imparted, in spite of the length of this letter, I mean only to write a simple note of gratitude and admiration. But my admiration does not have to do with your intellectual prowess. It does not have to do with the fact that you are a poet, or that you can build castles from

127

our ordinary language, or that you can penetrate the psychological mazes of the human mind to reveal its secrets, or that you have the unexcelled gift of dramatic dialogue which in your hands moves freely and unembarrassed, as informally as in a letter, but shot through and through with the deepest thought. My admiration refers to you neither as an aesthetician, nor as an ethicist, nor as a metaphysician, nor as a prophet. No, my admiration has to do with something else, something such that its very nature makes it impossible to admire directly, or establish through one's admiration any immediate relationship with you.[71] You have prevented this in your basic silence, your absence, your refusal to come forward publicly as the author of the work. I understand, Victor. I understand how, in your silence and withdrawal, you have left a space for each man to come forward in his own way, in his own time. Something strange begins to stir within me; something not wholly new but rather renewed, something from the old realm of despair of which I thought I had seen the last.

Though I long to know who you are, to know you intimately, to ask you in every possible way if you deliberately intended to evoke what response you did evoke in me, I understand and accept the fact that I can only thank you indirectly. Allow me to do so . . . and absolutely . . .

Your Reader

Johannes de Silencio and Constantine Constantius[72]
c/o Reitzel's
Copenhagen

Dear Johannes:

Do you like this name? But that is not the point. I understand the reason for the name, and so I shall address you as
"Johannes," though you must not imagine that your reader is so imperceptive as to misinterpret a voice so familiar;
or, for want of such perception, that he fails to read the
daily newspaper.[73]
     Since my experience with *Either/Or*, a book purchased
at Reitzel's, I have made it a point to pass the old man's
place each day, as a lover is irresistably drawn past the beloved's quarters, to be imbued with the climate in which
she lives, to sense her presence there, to anticipate some
new revelation, to hope for a chance meeting. So I have
daily passed the window of Reitzel's, peering into it, prepared for an encounter with some new mystery, entranced
by the expectation, the possible. Last week, with a kitchen
maid at my side (a habit which even impending despair can
not seem to break), it happened. For weeks, nothing but
the most unappetizing of titles appeared like pasteboard
cakes upon pedestals in the window. But that day, there
appeared amid *Garden Spice and Wild Pot Herbs*, *World's
Favorite Solos for Voice*, and a *New World Atlas*, two
small, unobtrusive books: *Fear and Trembling* and *Repetition*. "Yes! Here they are!" I thought, "The signs for which
I have been waiting!" It was like receiving two love letters
in the same post! The second and third ones — which deny
transiency and unfaithfulness, and which lift the lover up

over 70,000 fathoms. The very appearance of the two books engendered within me a deep sense of confidence which enabled me to restrain my excitement, to hold it patiently, secretly inside myself. The charming kitchen maid upon my arm did not, I am certain, sense the least digression of my attention from her; though my entire focus had shifted from her to you, from one form of seduction to another. At most, it was evident to her that I had "taken note" of something. And, oddly enough, the encounter took place while she was prattling about the town's current preoccupation: the love affair between the innocent and young Regine Olson and the brilliant but corrupt Soren Kierkegaard. What an explosion of thought and feeling I had to contain until I could return to Reitzel's and possess your new books.

I was certain that you would write again, and more; for I felt *Either/Or* to carry a promise made to me, your reader, that a work so prodigious, so involuted and yet so personally stinging and direct, whose existence was all the more remarkable because it was written in so inimical a context, would not be the last work. No. You could not abandon your reader without further word.

For many hours in a nameless cafe I sat reading the books. Undoubtedly, my fellow aesthetes were shocked at my resistance to the lure of their all-too-obviously heated company. Similarly, my kitchen maid must have come near to self-criticism upon my polite and prompt departure at her kitchen door. In the space between dusk and dawn, I I read both books. They are both true to form. Your voice is still yours; I hear you. And though I cannot yet explain or interpret your speech, I have added to the word, *despair* the words *sacrifice* and *repetition.* Dear Johannes! I can understand more, and far better when I relate these words to a certain love affair which has shaken the whole town than I can when the words remain in their fictional context. But you are too clever not to have intended this double reference. So be it. But can you know how well your words can be understood when they come into relation with my own life?

But I shall resist specificity. Here is a repetition from two sides! For you, too, fail to be specific; you, too, give no real information; you, too, remain fortified in inwardness. So, too, the most I shall confess, my Johannes, is a repetition: the Seducer lives! He catapults himself into existence each time he recognizes his own despair; this despair has brought him to the brink of an alternative; and over the distant stretches of sand which bound this alternative there hovers a possibility.

But. I have only been led to the edge of the desert. I have not yet been persuaded, I am not yet committed to pass beyond the city gate. Oh! But I should like to go with you! You are one with me in your distance. What a grand journey across the sands we should make, supporting each other in the paradoxes of our isolated missions, understanding each other in the sealed cloisters of silence, speaking words of love to each other in each step which sinks into the sand, loving each other in our devotion to the desert, being men in ways that men could never be. I should like to go with you . . . if only I could be sure you were going . . . if only I could be sure . . .

Do you long to know me as I long to know you? Will you write still another book?

Your lover

Dear Johannes, dear Vigilius:[74]

Not one, but two books! Not one, but two new personalities, expressing in two new ways your devotion. I do not read these two new books as I have read the last two — over and over again, like love letters expressing the first efflorescence of love. I dwell with the new books more soberly, with their resonant themes: sin and faith. They intoxicate me with rich implications, innumerable possibilities, with the multiplicity of tongues in which they speak. My life has been almost entirely changed! More and more do I seem to be held in patient waiting. But I do not know what I am waiting for. A decisive choice, perhaps. Can you believe that I spend my days hovering around Reitzel's in only apparent devotion to comraderie with those who, like me, come, in cafe-love, to search for the True and the Beautiful? Like you, I am an object of attention; indeed, I court attention in my every gesture. But my appearance is a ruse. I am at Reitzel's not to play the part of the frenzied aesthete. I am driven there by a secret obsession. I am a moth with transparent wings, fluttering around an empowering candle flame. Should you visit Reitzel's as a spy in search of me, you would find no clue;[75] as I, though my life is at stake in your authenticity, have been unable to make an unshakable identification of you. Like you, I am obvious, utterly revealed; like you, I am utterly private, a mirage; my being having no appearance; my appearance having no being.

But. Be assured of this much: you are my author and I am your reader. So I mull about, every so often peering into the display window anticipating the moment when I shall see in it more than my own reflection, for the moment when I can again commune with you in the only way open to us . . . through writing. My life seems now to center in writing; but ideas and words alone lack what power I need for change. All of the seductive patterns of my past still fail to come loose; they hang like dead oak leaves in winter, trembling with the cold winds but fixed in place all the same — the same social costumes, the same poetic flavors, the same temptations and desires, the same absorption in the moment, the same life swirling between the bedsheets in a kitchen maid's quarters — these, the dying, but sole signs of my hold upon life.

Yet, I wait. When will the bookseller's assistant place another communication from you in that window? I wait for the sight of his anonymous hands; and in my patient waiting, I lose, bit by bit, the power to hold to my former life. I am coming close to a decision, on the brink of a commitment to a new life. My mind reels beneath the weight of your ideas: despair, sacrifice, repetition, sin, and faith. I am dizzy from the looping dance of thought into which they have drawn me. Will I lose my hold only to be sent spinning into the abyss? Or will you be there, my new partner?

You cannot mean what you say about the dance.[76] I am your partner . . . so clearly at your invitation . . . and I return the invitation — Come! Dance with me!

That Individual

Dear Mr. Bogbinder: and associates:[77]

Oh! If you knew me! I am as unexpectedly your reader as you are my author. You would be . . . oh, yes! But what is even more shocking, what troubles me even more deeply, is my own self-estrangement. More and more frequently am I aware of my fragmented self. I move about as if a set of circular mirrors were appended to my extremities, expressing my presence in an endless flow of reflections. I no longer exist in the world self-identical or integrated with time. I flee the world haunted by you, by your intrusiveness, by your silent admonitions, by your relentless repetitions; or am I haunted by myself? What matter! We are both phantoms! For who are you? Who am I? Ah! But then it does make sense after all — it is the business of phantoms to be haunting! Perhaps an example, taken from the recent past, can break the spell. To tell of it, I must break our vows to remain unspecified; but then perhaps it will not hurt.

Just yesterday morning, my current flame stole away from her work in the kitchen of a town notable and approached me at my regular breakfast in the cafe. For weeks I suspect that I have been behaving most strangely toward her. It would not surprise me to learn that I hadn't seen her at all, for I do not have anything but the vaguest memories of the past weeks. She approached my table in great agitation; but sat down beside me without uttering one word. Quite suddenly, her shawl dropped from her shoulders,[78] almost completely exposing her breasts, which rested just above her lace-trimmed corset. The act bore a clear resemblance to the sort of response I would expect upon surprising her with a visit after work. She had obviously planned it, arranging the cloth in such a manner as to bring about the desired effect; the only difference was that this was a public, not a private act. It was extraordinary! But my response was truly extraordinary! What

134

did I proceed to do? I took another bite of my breakfast tart and a sip of tea.

Still she sat for many moments, bare-breasted beside me, apparently determined to remain waiting for a more suitable response. I might have made that response, but I was inwardly paralyzed by a certain brooding — not a melancholy, but a kind of absolute purification of feeling. I was just on the other edge of being a voluptuary — I had no feeling at all.

For some time now I have been unable to do anything whatsoever. I can't bother to get up; the strain is too great; I can't bother to rest; for either I would repose too long, and I can't bother to do that, or I would rise at once; and I can't bother to do that, either. There is little which is not too strenuous for my apathy. All I can bother to do, it seems, is to sit, vaguely picking at my food in a cafe, being gently rocked by the multitude of objects which glide past me and the trail of sterile notions which glide through me. In vain have I sought something that might enliven me. Even now, I can't bother to set down what I have just set down and I can't bother to cross it out.[79] The same was true that morning. I could not, as much as I willed it, infuse her or the situation with enough significance to marshall even a word, a gesture. I should have had to traverse an infinite gulf to do so. And I have already been to the place at which I should arrive. No. To respond to her would have been to blot out the possibility of a new revelation, to irretrieveably waste the energy needed to grasp it, and to commit myself to it.

After a while, I noticed that her breathing was becoming strained; and her breasts began to heave so violently as to threaten to create an embarrassing scene. Then, in a burst of tears which were at once angry, overweening, and humble, she asked, "Do you not like me at all?" and she tore a piece of paper which she had previously placed in the fold of her corset and offered it to me with the words, "You have made a fearful fool of me."[80] Though I probably would not have implored her to stay under any circumstances, she left before I had the chance to examine the paper. I cannot imagine what would have been sufficient to disturb me that morning; I am by no means a phlegmatic type. I was somehow anesthetized. Only after the last sip of tea did I read the paper which I had rather mindlessly set down next to the menu.

It was a Last Will and Testament; a self-composed, simple document inscribed at the top with the words, "Love is Everything."[81] I stared blankly at it; then, mechanically lifting my head, I stared hard at the sights before my eyes: the fluid movement of passers-by, the maid scouring in the yard, the groom currying his horse, carriages off to the country, shrimp vendors gesturing their wares away in distant cries,[82] clouds wafting along in the sky; and then the dense visions which brought this movement to rest, which blocked out the effluent sun and the distant, beckoning horizon; and I was relieved whenever my eyes reached some such limit; for my own soul had lost its bounds; it cared for nothing; it bore no fruit and received none . . . it drifted . . . a cruising, languid breakfast of soul, on vacation at sea.

I must have fallen into a trance, because I remember feeling as if I were on board a steamer going to Berlin.[83] I was the only passenger. It was close to dawn; and I was sitting alone at a table, eating breakfast. From my seat on deck, I gazed out into the heavy fog which had suddenly engulfed the harbor. All of the familiar outlines of Copenhagen receded into it, and, whisked upwards in a squall with them, one-by-one, flew all of those persons who, at one time or another, had passed through my life. As I sat, the fog became thicker, more and more aggressive, crowding the ship in its gossamer domination of the sea, wedging its way round and through the ship's open spaces. I suddenly became aware of the fog's approach toward me, and the claim to my own life which it was making. I would surely have allowed it to pluck me painlessly from my chair and whirl me away. But then, as suddenly as it appeared, the fog dissipated; and out of the clear, icy waters which bewitched it away there came an abysmal silence; there hung an inconceivable stillness like one might imagine existed before creation. In the midst of this silence and this stillness, I rose spellbound from my place on deck to become the first man who ever lived.

Then . . . what had just begun came to an abrupt end — a dream! It was all just a dream! It is all still a dream; a dream which rolls in again with the fog and out again in enchantment. What must be done to make it real? Surely I have understood the meaning of the *Stages on Life's Way* — for my resurrection has been foretold. Perhaps now I am offered a chance to accomplish more than can be expected from ideas and dreams. Beside me is a Last Will and Testament. The life of a woman waits upon my response. Her soul. My soul. Your soul. You must send me word. Am I to finish tomorrow's breakfast, too? How am I to know what must be done!?

That Individual

Dear Frater Taciturnus: [84]

It has been almost a year since my last letter to you. I had
given up the idea that communication with you had to
obey the law of an "eye for an eye." It would have been a
hopeless pursuit; I, spending the major part of each day
trying endlessly to catch up with my mail. But the practical impossibility of responding to you page by page was
not the critical factor in my long silence. What was required of me was not the speech which could reach the
ears of another man, but rather a wholly inward, silent action; not an attempt to identify with someone else (even
though he constituted the standard toward which I strove),
but an individual project with a reflexive reference.

So it has been almost a year since my last letter. During this year I have struggled almost continuously with the
great puzzles and possibilities presented by your books and
their radical effect upon my life. It was a fitful year; a year
of dark nights for my soul Unnerved and helpless, I had to
begin a retreat through ruined fields and ravaged plains surrounded everywhere by the sterility of desolation, by gut-
ted plans and smouldering ashes of hope twisted, of success blotted out and tranquil hours gone forever, a retreat
slow as Satan's wings, long as infinity, repeatedly interrupted by the mournful plaint: "I have no pleasure in
these days." [85] My life needed re-living; and such repair
means suffering; and suffering takes time. It takes time to
survey the ruins of the past and to find among them the
promise of a new future. Often I found myself on the
brink of this future, in the midst of a new revelation to
which I could commit myself; but just as often I found
myself stepping precipitously close to the edge of the

abyss, feeling in the arches of my feet the pains of holding ground. Too often, in response to the pain, I longed to make one last, agonizing leap. But I managed somehow to endure; not on the basis of any guarantee either subjectively projected or objectively offered, not on the basis of romantic imaginings, or upon imposed standards, not even upon an intoxication with the suffering itself. No. I held my ground on the basis of some intuitive but fleeting sense of support which came and went in equally unexpected moments. It struck me as strange that just when I had given up communicating with you directly, trying by this means to relieve my anguish by eliciting your personal support, I seemed to find your support that much more directly, despite the fact of its transience. In order for me to do what I had to do, to be enabled to do it, it was essential for you to maintain your pseudonymity, to remain concealed. Only upon this condition did I, and do I now, believe that I can make it, that I can come out on the other side of Time. It is critical that I sense the genuine possibility of a similar inward effort on the part of someone else. What your indirect yet unmistakable presence gives me is not hope, not proof, not even guidance . . . but the promise of love. Without this, I surely shall perish if I hadn't perished.[86]

But why am I now writing to you? There can be only one reason: my sense that my life, in its highest possibility, is being threatened by a false promise, perhaps (and I dread to think of it) a promise deeply misunderstood. This letter is an attempt to dissipate the threat; or if this cannot be done, to combat it. My soul is tormented by an article I have recently read in the *Corsair*, a newspaper in which I took great interest in the past because its scandalous, vulgar, unscrupulous, and absorbing content provided the material for the cafe life which sustained me as an aesthete. Though for the past year I have barely read the paper, I failed to discontinue my subscription. It was only the glaring familiarity of the caricature which appeared upon the front page which alerted me to it at all the other day. Seeing your image there in so public a context and so cruelly distorted was like being blackmailed without notice. Needless to say, I studied it and the accompanying account with attention to every detail. As I read, I sensed an impending calamity. The foreboding became even more emphatic when I discovered that you had responded to the article in the *Corsair* with your own article in *The Fatherland.*

I am anguished. I am terrified that you will feel the insult too sharply, and take offense so personally that you will be unable to remain silent. And yet I am already disconsolate that you have already betrayed yourself despite your use of the pseudonym. Your pseudonym! He does not even answer to his own name, but to the name of some other! I am in anguish; confused! But you seem more so than I! I fear this state. I fear that it is not the result of wounded pride which is expressed in spontaneous chaos, but that the chaos is the prelude to the madness of personal revenge. Take heed of my terror! I beg you!

I, a reader who loves you, could not persuade you out of hiding. Can the *Corsair* insult you into the open? Or is it really the crowd in the streets, those who spend only the time it takes to pass a rumor to know you, those whose illiteracy is justified by the filthy sheet, who will succeed in smoking you from their midst? If you should reveal yourself, I shall not have understood anything. What I heard as a promise will reduce to a muttering hallucination; what I once felt as a sense of kinship will become a mere charade. All will come to naught. I pray that my fears are ill-founded, that you will be stayed by the fatal consequence of revealing yourself. Our lives hang in the balance!

Your reader

Dear Victor, or Constantine, dear Johannes S or Johannes C, dear Vigilius or Hilarious,[87] dear Querilous or Perilous or Philias or sillyass, dear, dear KIERKEGAARD!!

If I have failed to make it indirectly clear by my treatment of the formal address, allow me to say directly, and in no uncertain terms, that I refuse to acknowledge your acknowledgment.[88] You *are* not Kierkegaard. I know your tricks, if no one else does. You have not been satisfied to wear the noble armor of Mars.[89] Invisibility bored you. But your new armor is no longer fashionable. You've lost your sense of public taste. Your newly chosen suit does not permit you to cross the threshold of appearance into the world of reality. It merely sounds a hollow, metallic clanging. You have succeeded only in adding a new alias, a queer new pseudonym: "Kierkegaard." "Kierkegaard," you would have your reader mutter to himself ponderously. What could this mean? "Churchyard?" Not quite. "Graveyard!" Yes, that's it! You shall hereafter be known as That Deceased Individual. The Dead and Departed One! How dare you make claim to the name of one living!? By a sleight of tongue to so suddenly change your tactics that you would switch missions. To presume to slip into the real world unnoticed . . . by murdering a real man and assuming his name! Yes. You are a murderer. We recognize you among us. No doubt, no ambiguity, no paradox about it at all. Can you believe us so dull as to be fooled by one who steals the crown of thorns, and then parades about like an escaped lunatic crying, "Bang! Kierkegaard lives!"[90] You differ only in degree from the worst criminal, romancing your guilt away, putting it at a distance by composing "A First and Last Declaration."[91] But since criminals are by definition, rather stupid and clumsy fellows (good! You are That Stupid and Clumsy Individual!), it is not surprising to find that their efforts at concealing their crimes result only in their dramatization. So fear not our retribution; for your own murderous soul will spit back at you and do the job (That Suicidal Individual!) So, I, your reader, who is no longer your reader, because you are no longer, has little to do to administer justice . . . oh, perhaps only to pull your hat permanently over your ears, making you[92] a statue of yourself, a walking-talking monument!

But first, I must reinstate myself: I have too long been a hesitant coward, suspending my bonds with men. Perhaps now, only through a woman, can I reclaim my humanity and justify calling myself a man. I may not even complete this letter before I rush to the place where she labors. And should she deny me entrance, I shall stand outside her door singing songs of love till she relents. And should she call the authorities, I shall insist upon an accusation face-to-face, during which I shall engage her in endless discussion of her motives till she surrenders. And should she attempt to strike me, or punish me in some other manner, I shall take her up into my arms and make these beating blows the rhythm of some new wedding dance. And if she should claim that she was already saved by the love of another[93] I shall weave that love into an enchanting fairy tale till it, too, becomes a fleeting illusion. And if there should be no time for all of this, if it should be too late, I shall do it all one night too early — by sorcery if need be. And when the deed is accomplished . . . and it shall be accomplished . . . I shall place her tiny hand, once too delicate to be mortal but made somehow more sacred in toiling for the rich, I shall place her hand upon mine as if this were a baptismal act, and together we shall promenade into the marketplace, appearing there in much the same way as in the past. People who knew us might remark to each other about our return; they may even deliberately pass close by, to greet us in welcome. To them, this repetition would be a restoration of normality. But they shall underestimate the meaning of our renewed presence. This promenade, unlike those of the past, shall have a singular goal, a mission if you will. We shall not leave the marketplace until we find you. When our paths cross . . . and they will cross . . . I, and my beloved, shall, quite playfully, join the rabble in the streets; join them in their chorus of deprecation, join with them in whispering beneath cupped hands, join in their finger-pointing and pasty grins.

And we may even attempt to go further; no; it will be unavoidable that we shall go further,[94] that we shall go 70,000 fathoms over and beyond[95] by spitting in your wake.

That Single Individual

1855 — 1972

'Write' — 'For whom' — 'Write for the dead whom thou didst love in the past' — 'Will they read me' — 'Yea, for they return as posterity.'

FEAR AND TREMBLING, *p. 12.*

Editor's Final Note

Once again, summer is gone. The grey barks of the distant beeches foretell winter. For me, at long last, the change of season rings true. Like a farmer or an animal in the wild, I had work to complete before the snows. Now I have done an honest job of it; of the work which once I wished would merely terminate, which then I regarded as a trap.

When I arrived at this cottage to begin my retirement, I thought I was through with Kierkegaard. When I discovered the rosewood box he left for me, I could not conceive ever being through with him. I might surely have become trapped by my own love, imprisoned by his seduction. I might, at most, have been able to renounce my love so to set it free (as SK himself claimed to do); or, perhaps, I might have been released by my own failure to love him as he insisted upon being loved. Then my fate as a lover would have been death. Surely each of the four persons whose love is reflected in the words I have edited suffered such a death. Each one of them tried, through love, to pull Kierkegaard into human life. Yet in each instance, the love which had to carry the burden of this seduction was far too concrete, too immediate, too real(!), to have been a genuine alternative to Kierkegaard's infatuation with Absolute Love. To plead that Absolute Love was and is *only* a possibility is only to strengthen Kierkegaard's attachment to it!

In the end, Kierkegaard sought death; for only death could accomplish what men could not. Only death could realize the possibility of Absolute Love. Only a longing for death could release SK from longing, could be a death to redeem death! And this was the promise of Christianity. Absolute Love for Absolute Faith! "Hallelujah!" he exclaimed as he moved toward death. His word epitomized his religious writing, his religious passion. Yet each of the religious words he wrote was a last word; and all of these last words were religious exclamations. Kierkegaard wished to live his whole life as a last sigh — a sigh of fire!

And yet . . . and yet he collected the fragmented papers of his mother, a prostitute, Regine, and a reader and left them for me! Why? Because these were the papers of his lovers, resonant with a language Kierkegaard could not learn, expressing a passion which could neither be fixed forever nor held fast in the moment nor transmuted by the imagination or intellect, Kierkegaard could not — would not — respond except in mere recognition. He could listen tentatively, but in the end the pure beauty of possibility transfixed him. As he surrendered to the promise of Absolute Love, his real lovers became only possible lovers — lovers of the dead. And yet . . . he collected the papers! This cannot be testimony to a hope for death!

In collecting and burying the papers of his lovers, Kierkegaard confessed, however secretly, both to an intention and to a failure to finish the work of love. His despair at having failed in love drove him to a new beginning in the collection of the papers. But then he buried them, because to do more than begin would have been to make the most terrible judgment of all upon his whole life!

Still . . . though SK ended his labor of love prematurely, he evidently did not intend to end it finally, for he buried the papers in the earth so that they could be resurrected, and he addressed them to that someone who alone could resurrect them — a lover! Yet so far as he knew, all his lovers had vanished. There was no one in particular to whom he could address them — no one, that is, whom he knew. But there were surely many whom he did not know, many who did not yet even exist! His past lovers were gone, but there were possible lovers yet to be! Despite his surrender to Absolute Love, and in the very grip of death, Kierkegaard could still hope to be heard by a possible human lover! It was surely as a possible lover that I read the words:

From One Who Was Left In A Sigh Of Fire
Upon Hearing His Lovers Vanish.

These words on a leaf of parchment were not buried in the earth to be taken by anyone — only by me. Only I could respond to the demand which Kierkegaard made through them — a strange, anguished plea that he be saved from that last sigh of fire by a possible lover become real. If, in the act of discovering these papers, I became a possible lover, I became a real lover only through my efforts to respond to the man who called me.

Of course, there were many other possible lovers who, real in their own ways, tried to keep Kierkegaard alive, too. There are, and will be, more! I have come to know only four, and have tried not to betray their love. But my faithfulness to them must disclose how each failed in love, and how their failures allowed SK to consummate his love affair with death which makes of men only possible lovers! The love of these four was unwitting, concrete, and immediate. They faltered before the dreadful task of competing with the possibility of Absolute Love; they were unable to lure Kierkegaard back from death. Each fails either by rejecting him or by surrendering to his rejection. I have had to allow them to fail, to become merely echoes of my own love. For my work cannot repeat theirs. I cannot allow SK the fulfillment that he longed for in courting their rejection, or by sacrificing his most dear so that love might be returned absolutely in death. In my work I cannot permit the death he thought would redeem him to destroy him. Not by default! The wittingness of my love permits me to recognize that Kierkegaard wished to be saved from that last sigh — and to respond to his plea in the redemptive fires of human passion.

And, oh, that no half-learned man would lay a dialectic hand upon this work, but would let it stand as it now stands!

CONCLUDING UNSCIENTIFIC POSTSCRIPT,
Acknowledgment.

NOTES

1. Soren Kierkegaard, *Stages On Life's Way* (New York: Schocken Books, 1969), p. 33.

2. Ibid., pp. 182-83.

3. Soren Kierkegaard, *Either/Or* (New York: Doubleday, 1959), I, 6.

4. Walter Lowrie, *Kierkegaard* (New York: Harper and Row; 1962), I, 59.

5. Kierkegaard, *Stages On Life's Way*, p. 249.

6. Soren Kierkegaard, *The Concept Of Dread* (Princeton, N.J.: Princeton University Press, 1967), pp. 109-21.

7. Soren Kierkegaard, *Repetition* (New York: Harper and Row, 1964), pp. 33-35.

8. Soren Kierkegaard, *The Point Of View For My Work As An Author* (New York: Harper and Row, 1962), pp. 75, 151. See also "Of The Difference Between A Genius And An Apostle," in *The Present Age*, Alexander Dru, trans. (New York: Harper and Row, 1962), pp. 89-108.

9. Kierkegaard, *Point Of View*, pp. 81, 90.

10. Ibid., pp. 75, 93.

11. The plight of Abraham is a good analogue to the struggles of Michael Pederson Kierkegaard.

12. Kierkegaard, *Stages On Life's Way*, pp. 236-37.

13. Kierkegaard, *Either/Or*, I, 4-6.

14. Walter Lowrie, *A Short Life Of Kierkegaard* (Princeton, N.J.: Princeton University Press, 1965), p. 44.

15. Kierkegaard, *Stages On Life's Way*, pp. 236-37 (Solomon's Dream).

16. Rudolph Friedmann, *Kierkegaard* (New York: New Directions, 1949), p. 34.

17. Kierkegaard, *Stages On Life's Way*, p. 182.

18. Lilies of the Valley were favorite gifts from SK to Regine.

19. This section can be read as an analogue to the four versions of the Abraham and Isaac story which appear in *Fear And Trembling.*

20. Kierkegaard, *Stages On Life's Way,* pp. 258-68.

21. Ibid., p. 257.

22. Ibid., p. 266.

23. Accounts of SK's Fall appear in Lowrie's *Kierkegaard,* p. 132, and Johannes Hohlenberg, *Soren Kierkegaard* (New York: Pantheon Books, 1954), p. 70.

24. Soren Kierkegaard, *The Diary Of Soren Kierkegaard,* Peter Rhode, ed. (New York: Philosophical Library, 1960), p. 13.

25. Kierkegaard, *Either/Or,* p. 310.

26. Soren Kierkegaard, *Fear And Trembling* (New York: Doubleday, 1954), pp. 27-28.

27. Ibid.

28. Soren Kierkegaard, *Soren Kierkegaard's Journals And Papers,* H. Hong and E. Hong, eds. (Bloomington, Ind.: Indiana University Press, 1970), II, 37.

29. T. H. Croxall, ed., *Glimpses and Impressions of Kierkegaard* (Hertfordshire, England; James Nisbet and Co., 1959), p. 9.

30. Kierkegaard, *Fear And Trembling,* p. 28.

31. Soren Kierkegaard, *Works Of Love* (New York: Harper and Row, 1964), p. 10.

32. Kierkegaard, *Fear And Trembling,* p. 28.

33. Ibid.

34. Ane Lund, SK's mother, was herself a distant relative and servant in the house of his father.

35. Kierkegaard, *Fear And Trembling,* pp. 28-29.

36. Ibid.

37. Croxall, *Glimpses and Impressions of Kierkegaard,* p. 66.

38. Soren Kierkegaard, *The Journals Of Soren Kierkegaard,* Alexander Dru, ed. (New York: Harper and Row, 1959), p. 115.

39. Kierkegaard, *Fear And Trembling,* p. 29.

40. Kierkegaard, *Journals,* Dru, ed., p. 42.

41. Kierkegaard, *Stages On Life's Way,* pp. 223-24.

42. Fritz Schlegel became governor of the West Indies after his marriage to Regine Olson.

43. SK commonly brought Regine gifts of music, books, flowers, and nuts.

44. Kierkegaard, *Either/Or*, p. 15.

45. Richard F. Burton, trans., *The Arabian Nights Entertainments* (New York: Random House, 1932), pp. 647–739.

46. Lowrie, *Kierkegaard*, p. 116.

47. Ibid., pp. 29–36.

48. This is an analogue of the journey made by Abraham and Isaac to Mount Moriah.

49. The problem of tarrying in moment, of time, is central to the tales of Don Juan, Faust, and the Wandering Jew; these heroes fascinated SK, who made extensive studies of and references to them.

50. Garden of Eden.

51. Hohlenberg, *Kierkegaard*, pp. 175–77.

52. See accounts of the spy in Kierkegaard, *Stages On Life's Way*, p. 94, and *Either/Or*, pp. 319–33.

53. Fritz Schlegel.

54. Kierkegaard, *Either/Or*, I, 314.

55. Hohlenberg, *Kierkegaard*, p. 231.

56. Kierkegaard, *Journals*, Dru, ed., p. 171.

57. Hohlenberg, *Kierkegaard*, p. 97.

58. Kierkegaard, *Stages On Life's Way*, p. 258. Knippelsbro was also a significant bridge, as it fronted Regine's house.

59. Kierkegaard, *Fear And Trembling*, p. 103.

60. Kierkegaard, *Stages On Life's Way*, p. 226.

61. The dilemma "guilty/not guilty" is the tortured theme at the heart of *Stages On Life's Way*.

62. Croxall, *Glimpses and Impressions of Kierkegaard*, p. 70.

63. Soren Kierkegaard, *The Concluding Unscientific Postscript* (Princeton, N.J.: Princeton University Press, 1964), p. 124.

64. Editor of *Either/Or*.

65. Hohlenberg, *Kierkegaard*, p. 16.

66. See the Seducer who appears in Vol. I of *Either/Or*.

67. Kierkegaard is presumed by some of his biographers to have Fallen by means of the sin of lust at twenty-three years of age.

68. This was to be Alaeddin's fate had he tarried in the seven halls.

69. This section of Carla's manuscript, indeed the work as a whole, can be treated as a repetition of SK's books (which are, presumably, repetitions of SK's life) but with a "twist."

70. SK asks for a reply from the owner of the rosewood box: Kierkegaard, *Stages On Life's Way*, p. 183.

71. Kierkegaard, *Concluding Unscientific Postscript*, p. 60.

72. Authors of *Fear And Trembling* and *Repetition*.

73. The conclusions that Kierkegaard was the author behind the pseudonyms was drawn and stated in the local newspapers.

74. Author of *Philosophical Fragments* and *The Concept of Dread*.

75. SK often described himself as a spy in a higher service, in much the same spirit as that of Socrates who often made reference to his own service to the Highest Good and to God.

76. Soren Kierkegaard, *Philosophical Fragments* (Princeton, N.J.: Princeton University Press, 1962), p. 7.

77. Bogbinder is the publisher of *Stages On Life's Way*.

78. Kierkegaard, *Stages On Life's Way*, p. 78.

79. Kierkegaard, *Diary*, Rhode, ed., p. 15.

80. Hohlenberg, *Kierkegaard*, p. 109.

81. Kierkegaard, *Either/Or*, I, 401.

82. Kierkegaard, *Diary*, Rhode, ed., p. 13.

83. Croxall, *Glimpses and Impressions of Kierkegaard*, p. 111.

84. Under this pseudonym, SK replied in *The Fatherland* to the article in *The Corsair*.

85. Kierkegaard, *Diary*, Rhode, ed., p. 13.

86. This saying modifies the saying "I had perished had I not perished" which SK derived from Hamaan (and Hamaan attributed to "A Greek"). It appears at the beginning of "Quidam's Diary," in *Stages On Life's Way*.

87. Kierkegaard, *Concluding Unscientific Postscript*, Acknowledgment.

88. Ibid.

89. Ibid., p. 730.

90. Ibid., p. 174.

91. Kierkegaard, *Diary*, Rhode, ed., p. 70.
92. Ibid., p. 79.
93. Fritz Schlegel.
94. Kierkegaard, *Fear And Trembling*, p. 132.
95. Kierkegaard, *Journals*, Dru, ed., p. 115.

KIERKEGAARD

A FICTION

has been composed in eleven point IBM Selectric
Century Medium, leaded two points and unjustified,
by Metricomp Studios; printed offset by Vail-Ballou
Press, Inc., on 55-lb. Sebago Antique paper;
adhesive bound by Vail-Ballou in Johanna Linson
over boards; and published by

SYRACUSE UNIVERSITY PRESS